FULL
METAL
JACKET

FULL METAL JACKET

The Screenplay by
Stanley Kubrick,
Michael Herr and
Gustav Hasford

With a Foreword by
Michael Herr

Alfred A. Knopf   New York   1987

Library of Congress Cataloging-in-Publication Data

Kubrick, Stanley.   Full metal jacket.
1. Vietnamese Conflict, 1961–1975—Drama.
I. Herr, Michael.   II. Hasford, Gustav.   III. Title.
PN1997.F78K83   1988   791.43′72   87-45979
ISBN 0-394-75823-4

Manufactured in the United States of America

FIRST EDITION

Based on *The Short-Timers* by Gustav Hasford,
published by Bantam Books

FOREWORD

I first met Stanley Kubrick in the spring of 1980, at his house outside London. It's nice to get a call from a culture hero, especially when you have so few. It isn't really true that Stanley Kubrick is a weird recluse, but it's usually true that if you're going to see him, you're going to his house, which is also his place of work, and business. We talked about many things that night, but mostly about war and movies. He had a strong feeling about a particular kind of war movie that he wanted to make, but he didn't have a story. By "story," I learned, he meant a book of such agreeable elements and proportions that he could break it down and build it up again as film; a tree with perfect branches. It was another seven years, a lot of it uphill, before he showed me the finished version of *Full Metal Jacket.*

I once told him about a dinner I'd had with a director who is at least as famous for his excesses as he is for his movies. We met to talk about a movie, but with one thing and another—mostly the dozen other people who joined us—the subject never came up, I know to our mutual relief. It was a star-studded table and a totally entertaining dinner, but dinner isn't work, necessarily. And as we left the restaurant, everybody checking out everybody else, I noticed roughly £300 of wine left at the table, all the bottles opened but otherwise untouched.

"There you go, Michael," Stanley said when I told him the story. "Those guys don't know how to live like monks."

And he does. He lives in a great house (great in the English, not the Californian, sense of the word), stocked inside with every toy a hyperactive technology can provide, but this is just a description of the physical plant. Most of the space, like the time, is for work. The action is strictly monastic, secular-electronic but ascetic. By temperament and through control (he is the control-freak *par excellence*), he conducts himself like a monk in the material world, disciplined and multi-disciplined. That's why his movies are his in ways no other American director can claim: Stanley Kubrick Presents a Stanley Kubrick Presentation. For someone who claims not to believe in the auteur, he makes extremely personal films.

During the next few years, we talked on the tele-phone. I think of it now as one phone call lasting three years, with interruptions. The substance was single-minded: the old and always serious problem of how you put into a film or a book the living, behaving presence of what Jung called the Shadow, "the most accessible of archetypes, and the easiest to experience." It was everywhere in Conrad's work, it starred in all of Buñuel's films, and it served as my personal co-pilot in Vietnam, where I learned to know and respect it. It came up out of me a thousand times to whisper the words spoken later by D.I. Sergeant Hartman in *Full Metal Jacket:* "I got your name. I got your number . . . Because I am hard, you will not like me . . . I am hard, but I am fair." Damned if you do, warped if you don't, that's what the Shadow thinks is fair. Only the courage to look it in the face can subdue it for even a minute, according to Jung, in so many words. War is the ultimate field of Shadow-activity, where all of its other activities lead you. As they expressed it in Vietnam, "Yea, Though I walk through the Valley of the Shadow of Death, I will fear no Evil, for I am the Evil." And the Fear, they could have added.

This is what we talked about in the eternal, recurring telephone call. Never boring, it was sometimes difficult. Talking to someone who is so blatantly hard at work can only mean that you are working, too. Writers stare at their tables all the time, and live such wonderful inner lives that they can forget to speak for days. In other words, most writers are manic-depressives, while movie directors are like generals, outward bound, out there and putting it out there, full of pep, talking story, brainstorming, performing schedules, highly conceptual, totally practical. This is compounded with Stanley by what I would have to call his intellectual fearlessness. His elevator goes all the way up to the roof. He's a regular mental warrior, and his means are telephonic. He has tremendous information, and he loves to process it. I valued his information so much that I didn't even charge him to talk to me. Nor did it matter that, after seven years' work on a Vietnam book followed by at least a year on a Vietnam movie, I wanted to become the last person in the world anybody would think of when they needed a Vietnam screenplay. So what money couldn't make me do, I did for information.

. . .

At the very moment in 1979 that I was making my No More Vietnams oath, I was sent a novel in bound galleys called *The Short-Timers,* by Gustav Hasford. I meant to read only a few pages, but I could see immediately, in one paragraph, that this was impossible. When I finished the opening section, I felt as though I'd read a whole novel, and it was twenty-eight pages long. I knew I was reading an amazing writer. He was telling a truth about the war that was so secret, so hidden, that I could barely stand it. I certainly didn't want to be associated with it in my neo-postwar period. It was a masterpiece that absolutely anybody could pick up and read in a couple of hours and never forget; and it went out into the world seeking shelf life without the albatross of my blurb around its graceful neck. I didn't answer the publishers, I didn't write to the author. I folded. I felt vaguely ashamed, but I got over it. I repressed it. Later, when Stanley was looking for war books, I may have mentioned it, but I'm not certain that I did. When he came across it, he knew immediately that he wanted to film it. I'd recoiled so far from it that I couldn't remember anything about it. It came straight back when I re-read that first great page.

I think that before he found the story and the locations, even before he knew which war he would be filming, he knew what the movie would look like. It was the leanness and incredible tact of *The Short-Timers* that was so satisfying. The dialogue wasn't like any movie dialogue we'd ever heard before. It was pre-cliché dialogue, the funniest and most painful distillations of the most extreme experience. The leanness was the story; lean young men, with only the teenage fat of their innocence to keep away the chill; and then they lose that. "The phoney-tough and the crazy-brave," walking the walk and slipping in blood, "Is that you John Wayne? Is this me?" The moral and political trellises are down, with all the rhetoric that grew on them. The audience would not be told how to watch this movie, nor which emotions they're supposed to be locating. This would be what the studios used to call a "Who Do You Root For?" movie, nonexplicit in its meanings, low-road in its production, minimal in expression; highly specific, like Hemingway. Simple surface, long reverberations.

Stanley wrote a detailed treatment of the novel. We met every day for a month and talked. We broke the treatment down into scenes, with a titled filing card for each scene. (One scene, the writer's dream, where the Lusthog Squad rests between battles, Iliad-style,

and talks and talks and talks, we called "C-Rats with André.") I wrote the first-draft screenplay from this, in prose form. The pages, if any, went out by car every afternoon, followed in the evening by a phone call. (Gustav Hasford says that one of his calls from Stanley ran more than seven hours.) If I got stuck, I'd phone that in, and Stanley would perform a line from his ongoing satirical revue of Hollywood types. "Don't write it fast, write it good," he'd say, in homage to Harry Cohn, and, "If it ain't broke don't fix it." (It's interesting, and often true, that scenes that are written fast usually play best.) When I finished the draft, he rewrote it, and I rewrote that. Gus came to London and wrote. Stanley rewrote all through shooting. Sometimes an actor, through inspiration or incapacity, would revise all of us. Lee Ermey, the ex-Marine who had been hired as technical advisor, bugged Stanley to test him for the part of Sergeant Hartman, and he brought a lot of his own incredible language in, like Orson Welles in *The Third Man.*

When Francis Coppola was making *Apocalypse Now* in the Philippines, the furies combined to turn the filming into something too much like Vietnam, and that was only part of what was paid for that great film. The furies would operate under tighter regulations on *Full Metal Jacket.* Except for some second-unit jungle footage, it would be filmed in England. He found Beckton, on Thames, an abandoned gasworks, and blew it up for Hue City. The cast was young, and used to short schedules. They heard that Stanley Kubrick worked his actors hard. They found out. Halfway through, when Lee Ermey was hurt in a car accident and shooting was suspended for three months, they really got salty. I went out a few times, by invitation. ("Hey Michael, wanna get your ass in the grass?") There's nothing more boring than a film location when you're not busy. It was a fairly tight ship, better than many, and there are plenty who would sail her again. Not exactly *frisson*-free, but that's the movies. Directors behave like directors, actors behave like actors, the jolly English crew behave jolly, and the writer watches. Stanley does not get lost on the set.

It takes a great manipulator to make a nonmanipulative movie. If you work as a writer on a movie, you inevitably shoot a version of it in your mind. Just as inevitably, the director will shoot a movie that is nothing like yours. Yours is in your head with no audience, and his is on the screen. Almost the first thing that struck me about *Full Metal Jacket* was how little it had to do with me. I suffered the usual screenwriter's losses, and found them acceptable losses. It was very different from Gus's book, but true to it. I couldn't, and can't, get over the beauty of the acting. And the next morning, I couldn't remember for a long time what I thought had been cut—lines that had been fun to write, whole scenes, beloved voice-overs, stuff that looked great on the page but couldn't be performed. I could only remember the completeness of the movie, and how new it looked to me.

When *Viva Zapata* came out in 1952, the ads featured a rave from John Steinbeck, something like, "The greatest movie of all time." I remember how I felt when I saw that John Steinbeck had also written the screenplay. Without the words to say it, I was shocked by the immodesty of it, the shameless conflict of interest. But I was only twelve then, and had never written for the movies. At least from the day that Stanley saw the phrase "full metal jacket" in a gun catalogue and found it "beautiful and tough, and kind of poetic," he had taken the book and the script, the cast and the technicians, into his obsession. We'd get out when the movie got out. Film isn't all that's released when a powerful picture is finished.

MICHAEL HERR
August 1987

FULL
METAL
JACKET

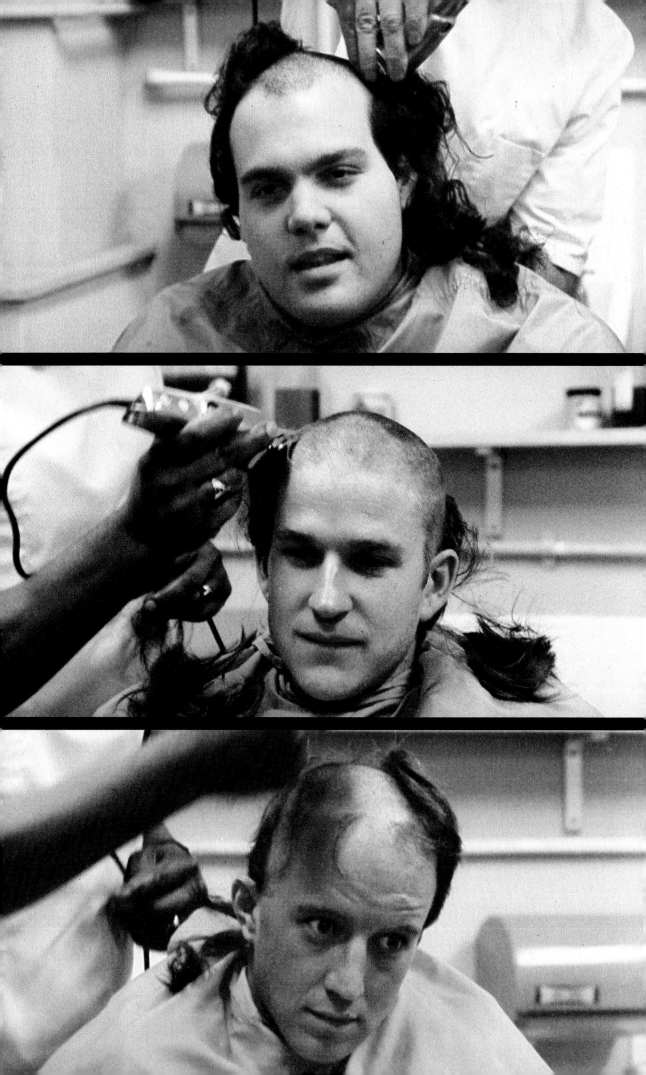

FADE IN:

WARNER BROS. LOGO:

WARNER BROS. PICTURES
WB
A WARNER COMMUNICATIONS COMPANY

LOGO FADES OUT:

Music: Johnny Wright's "Hello Vietnam"

TITLE: A STANLEY KUBRICK FILM

CUT TO:

TITLE: FULL METAL JACKET

CUT TO:

1 INT. BARBERSHOP—PARRIS ISLAND MARINE BASE—
DAY

Marine recruits having their heads shaved with electric clippers. The hair piles up on the floor.

2 INT. BARRACKS—DAY

Marine recruits stand at attention in front of their bunks.

Master Gunnery Sergeant HARTMAN *walks along the line of blank-faced recruits.*

HARTMAN
I am Gunnery Sergeant Hartman, your Senior Drill Instructor. From now on, you will speak only when spoken to, and the first and last words out of your filthy sewers will be "Sir!" Do you maggots understand that?

RECRUITS
(in unison)
Sir, yes, sir!

HARTMAN
Bullshit! I can't hear you. Sound off like you got a pair.

RECRUITS
(louder)
Sir, yes, sir!

HARTMAN
If you ladies leave my island, if you survive recruit training . . . you will be a weapon, you will be a minister of death, praying for war. But until that day you are pukes! You're the lowest form of life on Earth. You are not even human fucking beings! You are nothing but unorganized grabasstic pieces of amphibian shit!

Because I am hard, you will not like me. But

the more you hate me, the more you will learn. I am hard, but I am fair! There is no racial bigotry here! I do not look down on niggers, kikes, wops or greasers. Here you are all equally worthless! And my orders are to weed out all non-hackers who do not pack the gear to serve in my beloved Corps! Do you maggots understand that?

> RECRUITS
> *(in unison)*
> Sir, yes, sir!

> HARTMAN
> Bullshit! I can't hear you!

> RECRUITS
> *(louder)*
> Sir, yes, sir!

Sergeant HARTMAN *stops in front of a black recruit, Private* SNOWBALL.

> HARTMAN
> What's your name, scumbag?

> SNOWBALL
> *(shouting)*
> Sir, Private Brown, sir!

> HARTMAN
> Bullshit! From now on you're Private Snowball! Do you like that name?

> SNOWBALL
> *(shouting)*
> Sir, yes, sir!

> HARTMAN
> Well, there's one thing that you won't like, Private Snowball! They don't serve fried chicken and watermelon on a daily basis in my mess hall!

> SNOWBALL
> Sir, yes, sir!

> JOKER
> *(whispering)*
> Is that you, John Wayne? Is this me?

> HARTMAN
> Who said that? Who the fuck said that? Who's the slimy little communist shit twinkle-toed cocksucker down here, who just signed his own death warrant? Nobody, huh?! The fairy fucking godmother said it! Out-fucking-standing! I will P.T. you all until you fucking die! I'll P.T. you until your assholes are sucking buttermilk.

Sergeant HARTMAN *grabs* COWBOY *by the shirt.*

> HARTMAN
> Was it you, you scroungy little fuck, huh?!

> COWBOY
> Sir, no, sir!

> HARTMAN
> You little piece of shit! You look like a fucking worm! I'll bet it was you!

> COWBOY
> Sir, no, sir!

> JOKER
> Sir, I said it, sir!

Sergeant HARTMAN *steps up to* JOKER.

> HARTMAN
> Well . . . no shit. What have we got here, a fucking comedian? Private Joker? I admire your honesty. Hell, I like you. You can come over to my house and fuck my sister.

Sergeant HARTMAN *punches* JOKER *in the stomach.* JOKER *sags to his knees.*

> HARTMAN
> You little scumbag! I've got your name! I've got your ass! You will not laugh! You will not cry! You will learn by the numbers. I will teach you. Now get up! Get on your feet! You had best unfuck yourself or I will unscrew your head and shit down your neck!

> JOKER
> Sir, yes, sir!

HARTMAN
Private Joker, why did you join my beloved
Corps?

JOKER
Sir, to kill, sir!

HARTMAN
So you're a killer!

JOKER
Sir, yes, sir!

HARTMAN
Let me see your war face!

JOKER
Sir?

HARTMAN
You've got a war face? Aaaaaaaagh! That's a
war face. Now let me see your war face!

JOKER
Aaaaaaaagh!

HARTMAN
Bullshit! You didn't convince me! Let me see
your real war face!

JOKER
Aaaaaaaaaaaaaaaaaagh!

HARTMAN
You didn't scare me! Work on it!

JOKER
Sir, yes, sir!

Sergeant HARTMAN *speaks into* COWBOY's *face.*

HARTMAN
What's your excuse?

COWBOY
Sir, excuse for what, sir?

HARTMAN
I'm asking the fucking questions here,
Private. Do you understand?!

COWBOY
Sir, yes, sir!

HARTMAN
Well thank you very much! Can I be in charge
for a while?

COWBOY
Sir, yes, sir!

HARTMAN
Are you shook up? Are you nervous?

COWBOY
Sir, I am, sir!

HARTMAN
Do I make you nervous?

COWBOY
Sir!

HARTMAN
Sir, what? Were you about to call me an
asshole?!

COWBOY
Sir, no, sir!

HARTMAN
How tall are you, Private?

COWBOY
Sir, five foot nine, sir!

HARTMAN
Five foot nine? I didn't know they stacked shit
that high! You trying to squeeze an inch in on
me somewhere, huh?

COWBOY
Sir, no, sir.

HARTMAN
Bullshit! It looks to me like the best part of
you ran down the crack of your mama's ass
and ended up as a brown stain on the
mattress! I think you've been cheated!

HARTMAN
Where in hell are you from anyway, Private?

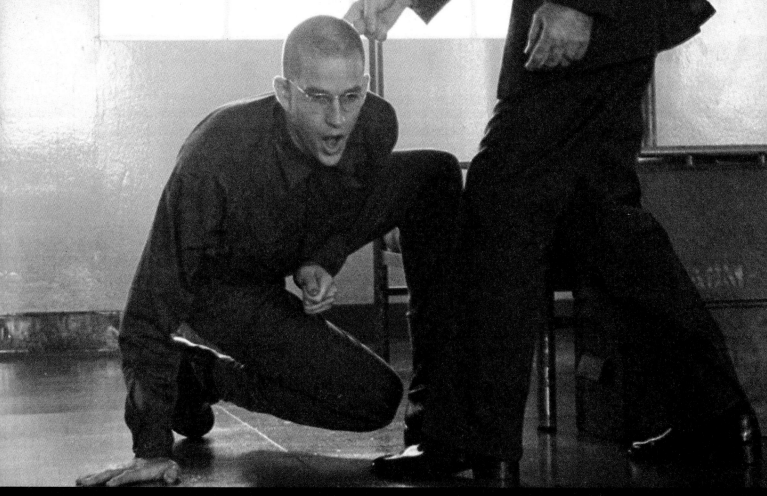

COWBOY
Sir, Texas, sir!

HARTMAN
Holy dogshit! Texas! Only steers and queers
come from Texas, Private Cowboy! And you
don't look much like a steer to me, so that
kinda narrows it down! Do you suck dicks!

COWBOY
Sir, no, sir!

HARTMAN
Are you a peter-puffer?

COWBOY
Sir, no, sir!

HARTMAN
I'll bet you're the kind of guy that would fuck
a person in the ass and not even have the
goddam common courtesy to give him a reach-
around! I'll be watching you!

Sergeant HARTMAN *walks down the line to another
recruit, a tall, overweight boy.*

HARTMAN
Did your parents have any children that lived?

PYLE
Sir, yes, sir!

HARTMAN
I'll bet they regret that! You're so ugly you
could be a modern art masterpiece! What's
your name, fatbody?

PYLE
Sir, Leonard Lawrence, sir!

HARTMAN
Lawrence? Lawrence, what, of Arabia?

PYLE
Sir, no, sir!

HARTMAN
That name sounds like royalty! Are you
royalty?

PYLE
Sir, no, sir!

HARTMAN
Do you suck dicks?

PYLE
Sir, no, sir!

HARTMAN
Bullshit! I'll bet you could suck a golf ball
through a garden hose!

PYLE
Sir, no, sir!

HARTMAN
I don't like the name Lawrence! Only faggots
and sailors are called Lawrence! From now on
you're Gomer Pyle!

PYLE
Sir, yes, sir!

PYLE *has the trace of a strange smile on his face.*

HARTMAN
Do you think I'm cute, Private Pyle? Do you
think I'm funny?

PYLE
Sir, no, sir!

HARTMAN
Then wipe that disgusting grin off your face!

PYLE
Sir, yes, sir!

HARTMAN
Well, any fucking time, sweetheart!

PYLE
Sir, I'm trying, sir.

HARTMAN
Private Pyle, I'm gonna give you three
seconds—*exactly three fucking seconds*—to
wipe that stupid-looking grin off your face, or
I will gouge out your eyeballs and skull-fuck
you! One! Two! Three!

PYLE *purses his lips but continues to smile involuntarily.*

> PYLE
> Sir, I can't help it, sir!

> HARTMAN
> Bullshit! Get on your knees, scumbag!

PYLE *gets down on his knees.*

> HARTMAN
> Now choke yourself!

PYLE *places his hands around his throat as if to choke himself.*

> HARTMAN
> Goddamn it, with my hand, numbnuts!!

PYLE *reaches for* HARTMAN's *hand.* HARTMAN *jerks it away.*

> HARTMAN
> Don't pull my fucking hand over there! I said choke yourself! Now lean forward and choke yourself!

PYLE *leans forward so that his neck rests in* HARTMAN's *open hand.*

HARTMAN *chokes* PYLE.

PYLE *gags and starts to turn red in the face.*

> HARTMAN
> Are you through grinning?

> PYLE
> *(barely able to speak)*
> Sir, yes, sir!

> HARTMAN
> Bullshit! I can't hear you!

> PYLE
> *(gasping)*
> Sir, yes, sir!

> HARTMAN
> Bullshit! I still can't hear you! Sound off like you got a pair!

> PYLE
> *(gagging)*
> Sir, yes, sir!

> HARTMAN
> That's enough! Get on your feet!

HARTMAN *releases* PYLE's *throat.* PYLE *gets to his feet, breathing heavily.*

> HARTMAN
> Private Pyle, you had best square your ass away and start shitting me Tiffany cuff links . . . or I will definitely fuck you up!

> PYLE
> Sir, yes, sir!

3 EXT. PARRIS ISLAND—DAY

The training platoon is double-timing in formation. HARTMAN *is calling cadence.*

> HARTMAN
> . . . right, left, right, left! Left, right, left, right, left! Left, right, left, right, left!

> JOKER
> *(narration)*
> Parris Island, South Carolina. . . . the United States Marine Corps Recruit Depot. An eight-week college for the phony-tough and the crazy-brave.

> HARTMAN
> Mama and Papa were laying in bed.

> RECRUITS
> *(chanting in cadence)*
> Mama and Papa were laying in bed.

> HARTMAN
> Mama rolled over, this is what she said . . .

> RECRUITS
> Mama rolled over, this is what she said . . .

> HARTMAN
> Ah, gimme some . . .

RECRUITS
Ah, gimme some . . .

HARTMAN
Ah, gimme some . . .

RECRUITS
Ah, gimme some . . .

HARTMAN
P.T. . . .

RECRUITS
P.T. . . .

HARTMAN
P.T. . . .

RECRUITS
P.T. . . .

HARTMAN
Good for you!

RECRUITS
Good for you!

HARTMAN
And good for me!

RECRUITS
And good for me!

HARTMAN
Mmm, good.

RECRUITS
Mmm, good.

HARTMAN
Up in the morning to the rising sun.

RECRUITS
Up in the morning to the rising sun.

HARTMAN
Gotta run all day . . .

4 EXT. PRACTICE FIELD — SUNSET

Recruits, silhouetted against the sun, climbing ropes, nets and ladders.

HARTMAN
. . . till the running's done!

RECRUITS
Gotta run all day till the running's done!

HARTMAN
Ho Chi Minh is a son-of-a-bitch!

RECRUITS
Ho Chi Minh is a son-of-a-bitch!

HARTMAN
Got the blueballs, crabs and the seven-year-itch!

RECRUITS
Got the blueballs, crabs and the seven-year-itch!

DISSOLVE TO:

5 EXT. PARADE DECK — DAY

HARTMAN *marches the platoon across a wide expanse of asphalt. The recruits carry rifles.*

HARTMAN
Left, right, left, right, left! To your left shoulder . . . hut! Left, right, left! Port . . . hut!

HARTMAN
Left, right! Platoon . . . halt! Left shoulder . . . hut!

PYLE *momentarily places his rifle on the wrong shoulder and immediately corrects himself.*

HARTMAN *spots this and walks up to him.*

HARTMAN
Private Pyle, what are you trying to do to my beloved Corps?

PYLE
Sir, I don't know, sir!

HARTMAN
You are dumb, Private Pyle, but do you expect me to believe that you don't know left from right?

PYLE
Sir, no, sir!

HARTMAN
Then you did that on purpose! You want to be different!

PYLE
Sir, no, sir.

HARTMAN *slaps* PYLE *hard across the left cheek.*

HARTMAN
What side was that, Private Pyle?!

PYLE
Sir, left side, sir!

HARTMAN
Are you sure, Private Pyle?

PYLE
Sir, yes, sir!

HARTMAN *slaps* PYLE *hard across the right cheek, knocking his cap off.*

HARTMAN
What side was that, Private Pyle?

PYLE
Sir, right side, sir.

HARTMAN
Don't fuck with me again, Pyle! Pick up your fucking cover!

PYLE
Sir, yes, sir!

DISSOLVE TO:

6 EXT. PARADE DECK—DAY

HARTMAN *marching the platoon—bringing up the rear is* PYLE, *his fatigue pants down around his ankles; he is sucking his thumb and he carries his rifle muzzle down.*

7 INT. BARRACKS—NIGHT

HARTMAN *walks along the line of recruits in skivvies holding their rifles and standing at attention in front of their bunks.*

HARTMAN
Tonight . . . you pukes will sleep with your rifles! You will give your rifle a girl's name! Because this is the only pussy you people are going to get! Your days of finger-banging old Mary Jane Rottencrotch through her pretty pink panties are over! You're married to this piece, this weapon of iron and wood! And you will be faithful! Port . . . hut! Prepare to mount! Mount!

On HARTMAN's *command the platoon mount their bunks with their rifles and lie on their backs at attention.*

HARTMAN
Port . . . hut!

The recruits snap their rifles to the port arms position over their chests.

HARTMAN
Pray!

RECRUITS
(in unison)
This is my rifle. There are many like it, but this one is mine. My rifle is my best friend. It is my life. I must master it, as I must master my life.

Without me my rifle is useless. Without my rifle, I am useless. I must fire my rifle true. I must shoot straighter than my enemy who is

trying to kill me. I must shoot him before he shoots me. I will.

Before God I swear this creed. My rifle and myself are defenders of my country. We are the masters of our enemy. We are the saviours of my life. So be it . . . until there is no enemy . . . but peace. Amen.

> HARTMAN
> Order . . . hut!

The recruits snap their rifles down to their sides.

> HARTMAN
> At ease!

HARTMAN *turns off the barracks lights.*

> HARTMAN
> Good night, ladies.

> RECRUITS
> *(in unison)*
> Good night, sir!

> HARTMAN
> *(to* DUTY GUARD*)*
> Hit it, sweetheart!

> DUTY GUARD
> Sir, aye-aye, sir!

8 EXT. PARADE FIELD—DAWN

HARTMAN *drills the platoon.*

> HARTMAN
> Right shoulder . . . hut! This is not your daddy's shotgun, Cowboy. Left shoulder . . . hut! Move your rifle around your head, not your head around your rifle. Port . . . hut! Four inches from your chest, Pyle! Four inches!

9 INT. BARRACKS—NIGHT

HARTMAN *marches the recruits through the squad bay. Their rifles are at shoulder arms and their left hands clutch their genitals.*

> HARTMAN
> This is my rifle! This is my gun!

> RECRUITS
> This is for fighting! This is for fun!

> HARTMAN
> This is my rifle! This is my gun!

> RECRUITS
> This is my rifle! This is my gun!

They repeat this over and over again as they march up and down the squad bay.

DISSOLVE TO:

10 EXT. PARADE DECK—DAY

HARTMAN *marching the platoon, calling cadence.*

11 EXT. "ARMSTRETCHER" OBSTACLE—DAY

Hand over hand the recruits swing along the "Armstretcher."

> HARTMAN
> Ten fucking seconds! It should take you no more than ten fucking seconds to negotiate this obstacle! Quickly, move it out! There ain't one swinging dick private in this platoon's gonna graduate until they can get this obstacle down to less than ten fucking seconds!

12 EXT. "TOUGH ONE" OBSTACLE—DAY

HARTMAN *watches as the recruits climb ropes and ladders to a high wooden tower above the platform.*

13 EXT. PUGIL-STICK CIRCLE—DAY

PYLE *and another recruit, wearing football-style helmets, batter each other with pugil sticks.*

The recruits are formed up around them in a circle. They cheer as PYLE *is beaten to the ground.*

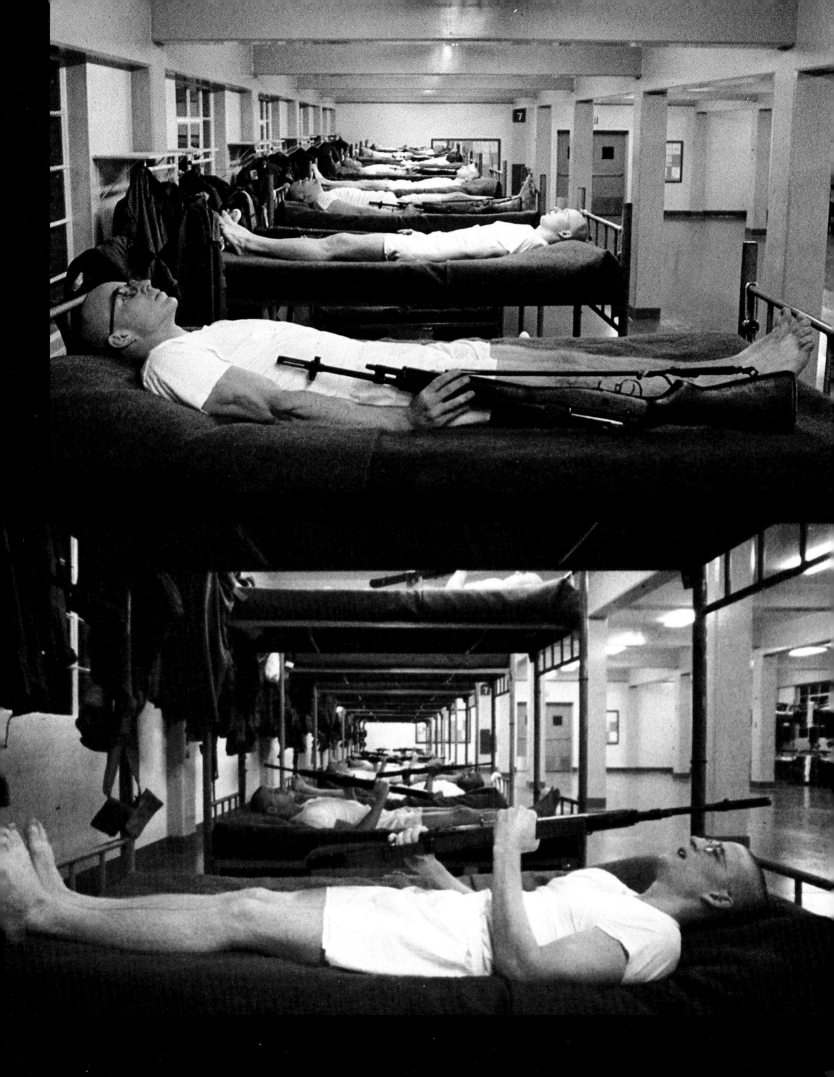

14 EXT. "DIRTY NAME" OBSTACLE—DAY

RECRUITS *waiting in two lines for their turn.*

> HARTMAN
> Next two privates! Quickly!

The next two recruits struggle over the obstacle.

> HARTMAN
> Get over that goddamn obstacle! Move it!
> Next two privates! Quickly! Hurry up! Get
> up there!

JOKER *and another recruit go over easily.*

> HARTMAN
> Private Joker, are you a killer?

> JOKER
> Sir, yes, sir!

> HARTMAN
> Let me hear your war cry!

> JOKER
> Aaaaaaaaaaaaaagh!

> HARTMAN
> Next two privates, go!

PYLE *and another recruit.* PYLE *is hopeless.*

> HARTMAN
> Quickly! Get your fat ass over there, Private
> Pyle! Oh, that's right, Private Pyle . . . don't
> make any fucking effort to get to the top of
> the fucking obstacle! If God wanted you up
> there He would have miracled your ass up
> there by now, wouldn't He?

> PYLE
> Sir, yes, sir!

> HARTMAN
> Get your fat ass up there, Pyle!

> PYLE
> Sir, yes, sir!

> HARTMAN
> What the hell is the matter with you anyway?
> I'll bet you if there was some pussy up there
> on top of that obstacle you could get up there!
> Couldn't you?!

> PYLE
> Sir, yes, sir!

PYLE *drops heavily to the ground.*

> HARTMAN
> Your ass looks like about a hundred and fifty
> pounds of chewed bubble gum, Pyle. Do you
> know that?

> PYLE
> Sir, yes, sir!

15 EXT. CHINNING BAR—DAY

Recruits are doing pull-ups. HARTMAN *watches*
JOKER *finishing many, many of them.*

> HARTMAN
> One for the Corps! Get up there! Pull!

JOKER *finally drops to the ground.*

> HARTMAN
> I guess the Corps don't get theirs. Get up
> there, Pyle!

PYLE *tries to do a pull-up but can't get to the top of
the bar.*

> HARTMAN
> Pull! Pull, Pyle, pull! One pull-up, Pyle! Come
> on, pull! You gotta be shitting me, Pyle! Get
> your ass up there! Do you mean to tell me
> that you cannot do one single pull-up?

PYLE, *exhausted from his efforts, drops to the
ground.*

> HARTMAN
> You are a worthless piece of shit, Pyle!! Get
> out of my face! Get up there, Snowball!

16 EXT. "CONFIDENCE CLIMB"—DAY

PYLE *climbs a high obstacle.*

> HARTMAN
> Get up here, fatboy! Quickly! Move it up!
> Move it up, Pyle! Move it up! You climb
> obstacles like old people fuck. Do you know
> that, Private Pyle? Get up here! You're too
> slow! Move it, move it! Private Pyle, what-
> ever you do, don't fall down! That would
> break my fucking heart! Quickly!

PYLE *freezes at the top.*

> HARTMAN
> Up and over! Up and over! Well, what in the
> fuck are you waiting for, Private Pyle? Get
> up and over! Move it, move it, move it! Are
> you quitting on me? Well, are you! Then quit
> you slimy fucking walrus-looking piece of
> shit! Get the fuck off my obstacle! Get the
> fuck down off of my obstacle! Now!

PYLE *climbs back down his side of the obstacle.*

> HARTMAN
> Move it! I'm gonna rip your balls off so you
> cannot contaminate the rest of the world! I
> will motivate you, Private Pyle, if it short-
> dicks every cannibal on the Congo!

17 EXT. ROAD—DAY

*The platoon is irregularly strung out on a road
nearing the end of a rapid, forced march.*

PYLE *is at the end of the line ready to drop.
Supported by* JOKER, PYLE *staggers along as*
HARTMAN *bellows at him.*

> HARTMAN
> Pick 'em up and set 'em down, Pyle!
> Quickly! Move it up! Were you born a fat
> slimy scumbag, you piece of shit, Private
> Pyle? Or did you have to work on it? Move
> it up! Quickly! Hustle up! The fucking war
> will be over by the time we get out there,
> won't it, Private Pyle?

HARTMAN *gives* PYLE *a shove.*

> HARTMAN
> Move it!

PYLE *gasps for breath.*

> HARTMAN
> Are you going to fucking die, Pyle? Are you
> going to die on *me!!* Do it now! Move it up!
> Hustle it up! Quickly, quickly, quickly! Do
> you feel dizzy? Do you feel faint? Jesus H.
> Christ, I think you've got a hard-on!

18 EXT. MUD OBSTACLE—DAY

The platoon tries to run through the mud. PYLE
half carried by JOKER *and* COWBOY *falls taking*
JOKER *down with him.*

> HARTMAN
> Quickly ladies! Assholes and elbows! Move it
> out! Get up there! Move it! Move it, move it,
> move it!

19 INT. BARRACKS—PRE-DAWN

HARTMAN *and two Junior Drill Instructors stride
into the Squad Bay. The lights go on.* HARTMAN
*bangs loudly on an empty metal garbage can which
he carries into the room.*

> HARTMAN
> Reveille! Reveille! Reveille! Drop your cocks
> and grab your socks! Today is Sunday! Divine
> worship at zero-eight-hundred! Get your
> bunks made and get your uniforms on. Police
> call will commence in two minutes!

HARTMAN *stops in front of* JOKER's *bunk.*

> HARTMAN
> Private Cowboy! Private Joker!

> COWBOY
> Sir, yes, sir!

JOKER
Sir, yes, sir!

HARTMAN
As soon as you finish your bunks, I want you two turds to clean the head.

JOKER & COWBOY
(in unison)
Sir, aye-aye, sir!

HARTMAN
I want that head so sanitary and squared away that the Virgin Mary herself would be proud to go in there and take a dump!

JOKER & COWBOY
(in unison)
Sir, yes, sir!

HARTMAN
Private Joker, do you believe in the Virgin Mary?

JOKER
Sir, no, sir!

HARTMAN *throws down the garbage can with a loud bang.*

HARTMAN
Private Joker, I don't believe I heard you correctly!

JOKER
Sir, the private said "No, sir," sir!

HARTMAN
Why, you little maggot! You make me want to vomit!

HARTMAN *slaps* JOKER, *hard, across the cheek.*

HARTMAN
You goddam communist heathen, you had best sound off that you love the Virgin Mary . . . or I'm gonna stomp your guts out! Now you do love the Virgin Mary, don't you?!

JOKER
Sir, negative, sir!!

HARTMAN
Private Joker, are you trying to offend me?!

JOKER
Sir, negative, sir!!! Sir, the private believes that any answer he gives will be wrong! And the Senior Drill Instructor will beat him harder if he reverses himself, sir!

HARTMAN
Who's your squad leader, scumbag?

JOKER
Sir, the private's squad leader is Private Snowball, sir!!!

HARTMAN
Private Snowball!

SNOWBALL *double-times up to* HARTMAN.

SNOWBALL
Sir, Private Snowball reporting as ordered, sir!

HARTMAN
Private Snowball, you're fired! Private Joker is promoted to squad leader!

SNOWBALL
Sir, aye-aye, sir!

HARTMAN
Private Pyle!

PYLE
Private Pyle reporting as ordered, sir!

HARTMAN
Private Pyle, from now on Private Joker is your new squad leader, and you will bunk with him! He'll teach you everything. He'll teach you how to pee.

PYLE
Sir, yes, sir!

HARTMAN
Private Joker is silly and he's ignorant, but

he's got guts, and guts is enough. Now, you ladies carry on.

> JOKER, COWBOY & PYLE
> (in unison)
> Sir, aye-aye, sir!

20 EXT. TRAINING FIELD—DAY

JOKER *patiently explains the disassembly of an M-14 rifle to* PYLE.

> JOKER
> The bolt. The bolt goes in the receiver. Operating rod handle. Operating rod guide.

21 INT. BARRACKS—NIGHT

JOKER *and* PYLE *sitting on their footlockers.* JOKER *instructs* PYLE *in the correct method of lacing his combat boots.*

> JOKER
> And the left one . . . over the right. Right one over the left. Left one over the right. Right one over the left.

22 EXT. CONFIDENCE CLIMB—DAY

On top of the confidence climb, JOKER *gently talks* PYLE *over the top.*

> JOKER
> Just throw your other leg over . . . that'a boy. That's it. Now just pull the next one over . . . and you're home free. Ready? Just throw it over. That'a boy. Just set it down. All right?

PYLE *breathes heavily. He is scared but he manages to get over.*

> JOKER
> There you go. Congratulations, Leonard. You did it.

23 INT. BARRACKS—NIGHT

JOKER *instructs* PYLE *in the correct way of making his bed.*

> JOKER
> You fold the blanket and the sheet back together. Make a four-inch fold. Okay? Got it? You do it.

PYLE *looks down uncertainly at the bed.*

24 EXT. PARADE DECK—DAY

JOKER *works with* PYLE *on the Manual of Arms.*

25 EXT. OBSTACLE COURSE—DAY

COWBOY, JOKER *and* PYLE *run up a ramp, grab the ropes and swing across a ditch.* PYLE *makes it without trouble.*

26 EXT. PARADE DECK—DAY

HARTMAN *is drilling the squad, calling the cadence and watching* PYLE *who makes no mistakes.*

DISSOLVE TO:

27 EXT. RIFLE RANGE—DAY

Targets are raised and lowered, red markers indicating hits. HARTMAN *addresses the recruits.*

> HARTMAN
> The deadliest weapon in the world is a marine and his rifle. It is your killer instinct which must be harnessed if you expect to survive in combat. Your rifle is only a tool. It is a hard heart that kills. If your killer instincts are not clean and strong you will hesitate at the moment of truth. You will not kill. You

will become dead marines. And then you will be in a world of shit. Because marines are not allowed to die without permission! Do you maggots understand?

> RECRUITS
> Sir, yes, sir!

28 EXT. PARRIS ISLAND STREET—DAY

The recruits are double-timing to HARTMAN's *cadences.*

> HARTMAN
> *(chanting in cadence)*
> I love working for Uncle Sam!

> RECRUITS
> *(chanting in cadence)*
> I love working for Uncle Sam!

> HARTMAN
> Lets me know just who I am!

> RECRUITS
> Lets me know just who I am!

> HARTMAN
> One, two, three, four! United States Marine Corps!

> RECRUITS
> One, two, three, four! United States Marine Corps!

> HARTMAN
> One, two, three, four! I love the Marine Corps!

> RECRUITS
> One, two, three, four! I love the Marine Corps.

> HARTMAN
> My Corps!

> RECRUITS
> My Corps!

> HARTMAN
> Your Corps!

> RECRUITS
> Your Corps!

> HARTMAN
> Our Corps!

> RECRUITS
> Our Corps!

> HARTMAN
> Marine Corps!

> RECRUITS
> Marine Corps!

> HARTMAN
> I don't know, but I've been told.

> RECRUITS
> I don't know, but I've been told.

> HARTMAN
> Eskimo pussy is mighty cold!

> RECRUITS
> Eskimo pussy is mighty cold!

> HARTMAN
> Mmm, good!

> RECRUITS
> Mmm, good!

> HARTMAN
> Feels good!

> RECRUITS
> Feels good!

> HARTMAN
> Is good!

> RECRUITS
> Is good!

> HARTMAN
> Real good!

RECRUITS
Real good!

HARTMAN
Tastes good!

RECRUITS
Tastes good!

HARTMAN
Mighty good!

RECRUITS
Mighty good!

HARTMAN
Good for you!

RECRUITS
Good for you!

HARTMAN
Good for me!

RECRUITS
Good for me!

29 INT. BARRACKS—NIGHT

The recruits in their skivvies stand at attention in two facing rows on top of their footlockers, arms outstretched, hands held rigidly in front of them, palms down, for inspection.

HARTMAN *moves along the row of men. He smacks a recruit's hand.*

HARTMAN
Trim 'em.

HARTMAN *points at the feet of another recruit.*

HARTMAN
Toejam!

To another recruit.

HARTMAN
Pop that blister!

HARTMAN *stops in front of* PYLE *and notices his footlocker is unlocked. He picks up the lock and holds it up to* PYLE.

HARTMAN
Jesus H. Christ! Private Pyle, why is your footlocker unlocked?

PYLE
Sir, I don't know, sir!

HARTMAN
Private Pyle, if there is one thing in this world that I hate, it is an unlocked footlocker! You know that, don't you?

PYLE
Sir, yes, sir!

HARTMAN
If it wasn't for dickheads like you, there wouldn't be any thievery in this world, would there?

PYLE
Sir, no, sir!

HARTMAN
Get down!

PYLE *steps down from the footlocker.* HARTMAN *flips open the lid with a bang and begins rummaging through the box.*

HARTMAN
Well, now . . . let's just see if there's anything missing!

HARTMAN *freezes. He reaches down and slowly picks up a jelly doughnut, holding it in disgust at arm's length with his fingertips.*

HARTMAN
Holy Jesus! What is that? What is that, Private Pyle?!

PYLE
Sir, a jelly doughnut, sir!

HARTMAN
A jelly doughnut?!

PYLE
Sir, yes, sir!

HARTMAN
How did it get here?

PYLE
Sir, I took it from the mess hall, sir!

HARTMAN
Is chow allowed in the barracks, Private Pyle?

PYLE
Sir, no, sir!

HARTMAN
Are you allowed to eat jelly doughnuts,
Private Pyle?

PYLE
Sir, no, sir!

HARTMAN
And why not, Private Pyle?

PYLE
Sir, because I'm too heavy, sir!

HARTMAN
Because you are a disgusting fatbody, Private
Pyle!

PYLE
Sir, yes, sir!

HARTMAN
Then why did you hide a jelly doughnut in
your footlocker, Private Pyle?

PYLE
Sir, because I was hungry, sir!

HARTMAN
Because you were hungry?

Holding out the jelly doughnut, HARTMAN *walks
down the row of recruits still standing with their
arms outstretched.*

HARTMAN
Private Pyle has dishonored himself and

dishonored the platoon! I have tried to help
him, but I have failed! I have failed because
you have not helped me! You people have not
given Private Pyle the proper motivation!
So, from now on, whenever Private Pyle
fucks up, I will not punish him, I will punish
all of you! And the way I see it, ladies, you
owe me for one jelly doughnut! Now, get on
your faces!

HARTMAN
(to PYLE)
Open your mouth!

He shoves the jelly doughnut into PYLE's *mouth.*

HARTMAN
They're paying for it, you eat it!

HARTMAN *turns to the recruits.*

HARTMAN
Ready . . . exercise!

The platoon does push-ups.

RECRUITS
(chanting in cadence)
One, two, three, four!
I love the Marine Corps!
One, two, three, four!
I love the Marine Corps!
One, two, three, four!
I love the Marine Corps!
One, two, three, four . . .

While the platoon does push-ups, PYLE *swallows
hard to get down bites of the doughnut.*

DISSOLVE TO:

30 INT. BARRACKS—DAWN

JOKER *checks* PYLE's *uniform.*

JOKER
(quietly)
You really look like shit today, Leonard.

33

PYLE
Joker? Everybody hates me now. Even you.

JOKER
Nobody hates you, Leonard. You just keep making mistakes, getting everybody in trouble.

PYLE
I can't do anything right. I need help.

JOKER
I'm trying to help you, Leonard. I'm really trying.

PYLE *grins, trustingly.*

JOKER
Tuck your shirt in.

DISSOLVE TO:

31 EXT. TRAINING FIELD — DAY

The platoon does squat thrusts as PYLE *sits, his cap on backwards, sucking his thumb.* HARTMAN *watches.*

RECRUITS
(counting in unison)
One, two, three . . . nineteen!
One, two, three . . . twenty!
One, two, three . . . twenty-one!
One, two, three . . . twenty-two!
One, two, three . . . twenty-three!
One, two, three . . . twenty-four!
One, two, three . . . twenty-five!
One, two, three . . . twenty-six!
One, two, three . . . twenty-seven!
One, two, three . . . twenty-eight!
One, two, three . . . twenty-nine!
One, two, three . . . thirty!

FADE TO BLACK

32 INT. BARRACKS — NIGHT

We see a towel on a bed. A bar of soap is tossed

on the towel. The towel is folded over the soap forming a weapon.

A hand picks up the towel-weapon and bangs it on the mattress making a dull thud.

PYLE *is asleep in his bunk.*

The platoon silently slip out of their beds and form up around PYLE.

A blanket is thrown over PYLE, *each corner held down by a recruit, pinning* PYLE *to the bed.*

COWBOY *shoves a gag in* PYLE'S *mouth.*

PYLE *is helpless.*

The platoon files past beating PYLE *with the bars of soap wrapped in towels.*

PYLE'S *screams are muffled by the gag.*

JOKER *is the last one. He stands back from the bed.*

COWBOY
(to JOKER*)*
Do it! Do it!

JOKER *hesitates, then moves forward and hits* PYLE *hard several times.*

Then JOKER *jumps into his bunk.*

The recruits yank the restraining blanket off PYLE *and run back to their bunks.*

COWBOY
(removing gag)
Remember, it's just a bad dream, fatboy.

PYLE *sobs loudly and sits up, holding himself in pain.*

Lying in his bunk, JOKER *covers his ears.*

FADE IN:

33 EXT. PARADE DECK — DAY

The platoon is lined up.

HARTMAN
Port . . . hut! Left shoulder . . . hut! Right
shoulder . . . hut! Port . . . hut! Do we love
our beloved Corps, ladies?

RECRUITS
(shouting in unison)
Semper fi, do or die! Gung ho, gung ho,
gung ho!

PYLE *says nothing, just stares straight ahead.*

HARTMAN
What makes the grass grow?

RECRUITS
Blood, blood, blood!

PYLE *stares. Does not join in the shouting.*

HARTMAN
What do we do for a living, ladies?

RECRUITS
Kill, kill, kill!

PYLE *remains silent.*

HARTMAN
I can't hear you!

RECRUITS
Kill, kill, kill!

HARTMAN
Bullshit! I still can't hear you!

RECRUITS
Kill, kill, kill!

PYLE *continues to stare blankly ahead.*

34 EXT. BLEACHERS—DAY

The platoon sits on bleachers facing HARTMAN.

HARTMAN
Do any of you people know who Charles
Whitman was?

No response.

HARTMAN
None of you dumbasses knows?

COWBOY *raises his hand.*

HARTMAN
Private Cowboy?

COWBOY
Sir, he was that guy who shot all those people
from that tower in Austin, Texas, sir!

HARTMAN
That's affirmative. Charles Whitman killed
twenty people from a twenty-eight-storey
observation tower at the University of Texas
from distances up to four hundred yards.

HARTMAN *looks around.*

HARTMAN
Anybody know who Lee Harvey Oswald was?

Almost everybody raises his hand.

HARTMAN
Private Snowball?

SNOWBALL
Sir, he shot Kennedy, sir!

HARTMAN
That's right, and do you know how far away
he was?

SNOWBALL
Sir, it was pretty far! From that book
suppository building, sir!

The recruits laugh at "suppository."

HARTMAN
All right, knock it off! Two hundred and fifty
feet! He was two hundred and fifty feet away
and shooting at a moving target. Oswald got
off three rounds with an old Italian bolt action
rifle in only six seconds and scored two hits,
including a head shot! Do any of you people

know where these individuals learned to
shoot?

JOKER *raises his hand.*

> HARTMAN
> Private Joker?

> JOKER
> Sir, in the *Marines,* sir!

> HARTMAN
> In the *Marines!* Outstanding! Those
> individuals showed what one motivated
> marine and his rifle can do! And before you
> ladies leave my island, you will be able to
> do the same thing!

Camera slowly moves in on PYLE *staring at*
HARTMAN.

35 INT. BARRACKS—DAY

Recruits standing at attention in two facing rows.
HARTMAN *walks between the rows, leading them
in song.*

> HARTMAN & RECRUITS
> *Happy Birthday to you,*
> *Happy Birthday to you,*
> *Happy Birthday, dear Jesus,*
> *Happy Birthday to you!*

> HARTMAN
> Today . . . is Christmas! There will be a
> magic show at zero-nine-thirty! Chaplain
> Charlie will tell you about how the free
> world *will* conquer Communism with the
> aid of God and a few marines!
>
> God has a hard-on for marines because we
> kill everything we see! He plays His games,
> we play ours! To show our appreciation for
> so much power, we keep heaven packed
> with fresh souls! God was here before the
> Marine Corps! So you can give your heart
> to Jesus, but your ass belongs to the Corps!
> Do you ladies understand?

> RECRUITS
> Sir, yes, sir!

> HARTMAN
> I can't hear you!

> RECRUITS
> Sir, yes, sir!

36 INT. BARRACKS—NIGHT

*The recruits are seated on footlockers, cleaning their
rifles.* HARTMAN *prowls among them, watching.*

PYLE *talks softly to his rifle.*

JOKER *looks at him uneasily.*

> PYLE
> *(to his rifle)*
> It's been swabbed. . . . and wiped. Everything
> is clean. Beautiful. So that it slides perfectly.
> Nice. Everything cleaned. Oiled. So that your
> action is beautiful. Smooth, Charlene.

DISSOLVE TO:

37 INT. BARRACKS—NIGHT

A few recruits, including PYLE, *are mopping the
floor.*

38 INT. LATRINE—NIGHT

In the latrine COWBOY *and* JOKER *are also mopping
the floor.*

JOKER *stops, looks around to be sure they are alone,
and turns to* COWBOY.

> JOKER
> Leonard talks to his rifle.

COWBOY *keeps mopping.*

COWBOY
Yeah!

JOKER
I don't think Leonard can hack it anymore. I think Leonard's a Section Eight.

Pause.

COWBOY
It don't surprise me.

They both go back to mopping.

JOKER *speaks again after some silence.*

JOKER
I want to slip my tubesteak into your sister. What'll you take in trade?

COWBOY
What have you got?

39 EXT. FIRING RANGE—DAY

HARTMAN *kneels behind* PYLE, *looking on with approval.*

PYLE *finishes a good group and reloads his M-14.*

HARTMAN
Outstanding, Private Pyle! I think we've finally found something that you do well!

PYLE
Sir, yes, sir!

40 EXT. PARADE DECK—DAY

HARTMAN *inspects the recruits.*

HARTMAN
(to JOKER)
What's your sixth General Order?

JOKER
Sir, the private's sixth general order is to receive and obey and to pass on to the sentry

who relieves me . . . all orders . . . Sir, the private's sixth . . . Sir, the private has been instructed but he does not know, sir!

HARTMAN
You slimy scumbag, get on your face and give me twenty-five!

JOKER
Sir, aye-aye, sir!

HARTMAN *walks to* PYLE.

HARTMAN
How many counts in that movement you've just executed?

PYLE
Sir, four counts, sir!

HARTMAN
What's the idea of looking down in the chamber?

PYLE
Sir, that is the guarantee that the private is not giving the inspecting officer a loaded weapon, sir!

HARTMAN
What's your fifth general order?

PYLE
Sir, the private's fifth general order is to quit my post only when properly relieved, sir!

HARTMAN
What's this weapon's name, Private Pyle?

PYLE
Sir, the private's weapon's name is Charlene, sir.

HARTMAN
Private Pyle, you are definitely born again hard! Hell, I may even allow you to serve as a rifleman in my beloved Corps.

PYLE
Sir, yes, sir!

41 EXT. PARRIS ISLAND STREET—DAY

HARTMAN *double-timing the recruits, calling cadence.*

> HARTMAN
> I don't want no teenage queen.

> RECRUITS
> I don't want no teenage queen.

> HARTMAN
> I just want my M-14.

> RECRUITS
> I just want my M-14.

> HARTMAN
> If I die in the combat zone.

> RECRUITS
> If I die in the combat zone.

> HARTMAN
> Box me up and ship me home.

> RECRUITS
> Box me up and ship me home.

> HARTMAN
> Pin my medals upon my chest.

> RECRUITS
> Pin my medals upon my chest.

> HARTMAN
> Tell my mom I've done my best.

> RECRUITS
> Tell my mom I've done my best.

DISSOLVE TO:

42 EXT. FOREST—DAY

Woods. For the first time the platoon marches in full combat gear carrying rifles.

> JOKER
> *(narration)*
> Graduation is only a few days away and the recruits of platoon thirty-ninety-two are salty. They are ready to eat their own guts and ask for seconds.

43 EXT. FIELD—DAY

In full combat gear and with fixed bayonets, the recruits charge through green smoke.

> JOKER
> *(narration)*
> The drill instructors are proud to see that we are growing beyond their control. The Marine Corps does not want robots. The Marine Corps wants killers. The Marine Corps wants to build indestructible men, men without fear.

44 INT. BARRACKS—DAY

HARTMAN *talks to the recruits formed up in a school-circle.*

> HARTMAN
> Today you people are no longer maggots. Today you are marines. You're part of a brotherhood.

45 EXT. PARADE GROUND—DAY

Graduation. A marching band. Spectators. Hundreds of marines parade by in dress uniform.

> HARTMAN
> *(voice over)*
> From now on, until the day you die, wherever you are, every marine is your brother. Most of you will go to Vietnam. Some of you will not come back. But always remember this: marines die, that's what we're here for! But the Marine Corps lives forever. And that means *you* live forever!

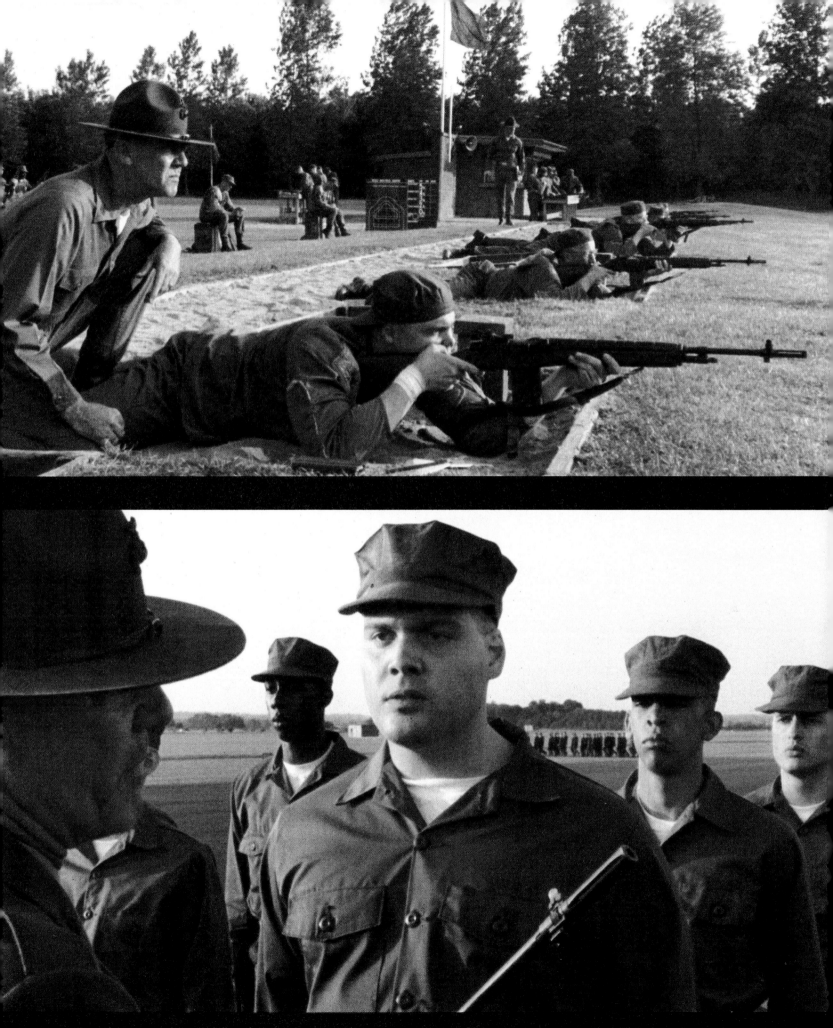

DISSOLVE TO:

46 INT. BARRACKS—DAY

HARTMAN *talks to the platoon, again in a school-circle.*

> HARTMAN
> Pickett!

> PICKETT
> Sir, yes, sir!

> HARTMAN
> O-three-hundred, Infantry. Toejam!

> TOEJAM
> Sir, yes, sir!

> HARTMAN
> O-three-hundred, Infantry. Adams!

> ADAMS
> Sir, yes, sir!

> HARTMAN
> Eighteen-hundred, Engineers. You go out and find mines. Cowboy!

> COWBOY
> Sir, yes, sir!

> HARTMAN
> O-three-hundred, Infantry! Taylor!

> TAYLOR
> Sir, yes, sir!

> HARTMAN
> O-three-hundred, Infantry. Joker!

> JOKER
> Sir, yes, sir!

> HARTMAN
> Forty-two-twelve, Basic Military Journalism. You gotta be shitting me, Joker! You think you're Mickey Spillane? Do you think you're some kind of fucking writer?

> JOKER
> Sir, I wrote for my high school newspaper, sir!

> HARTMAN
> Jesus H. Christ, you're not a writer, you're a killer!

> JOKER
> A killer, yes, sir!

> HARTMAN
> Gomer Pyle!

PYLE *doesn't answer.*

> HARTMAN
> Gomer Pyle!

We see PYLE *in close-up, now completely withdrawn, barely able to answer* HARTMAN.

> PYLE
> Sir, yes, sir!

> HARTMAN
> You forget your fucking name? O-three-hundred, Infantry. You made it. Perkins!

> PERKINS
> Sir, yes, sir!

47 INT. BARRACKS—NIGHT

The platoon sleeps. JOKER *walks slowly down the squad bay with a flashlight.*

> JOKER
> (narration)
> Our last night on the island. I draw fire watch.

JOKER *hears a muffled sound. He isn't sure where it comes from. He slowly enters the latrine.*

48 INT. LATRINE—NIGHT

Running his flashlight across the room JOKER *sees* PYLE *sitting on a toilet, loading a magazine for his M-14 rifle.*

PYLE *looks up at* JOKER *and smiles. It is a frightening smile.*

PYLE
(strange voice)
Hi, Joker.

JOKER *stares at* PYLE *for a few seconds.*

PYLE *has quite clearly snapped.*

JOKER
Are those . . . live rounds?

PYLE
Seven-six-two millimeter, full metal jacket.

PYLE *smiles grotesquely.*

JOKER
Leonard . . . if Hartman comes in here and catches us, we'll both be in a world of shit.

PYLE
I *am* . . . in a world . . . of shit!

PYLE *gets to his feet, snaps his rifle to port arms, and starts executing the Manual of Arms.*

PYLE
(shouting)
Left shoulder . . . hut! Right shoulder . . . hut! Lock and load! Order . . . hut!

PYLE *picks up the loaded magazine, inserts it into the rifle and smartly brings the rifle down to the order arms position.*

PYLE
(shouting)
This is my rifle! There are many like it, but this one is mine.

49   INT. BARRACKS HALLWAY—NIGHT

By now the platoon is awake.

HARTMAN *bursts from his room, wearing his skivvies and D.I. hat.*

PYLE
(offscreen)
My rifle is my best friend! It is my life!

HARTMAN
Get back in your bunks!

PYLE
(o.s.)
I must master it as I must master my life! Without me . . .

50   INT. LATRINES—NIGHT

HARTMAN *storms into the latrine.*

HARTMAN
What is this Mickey Mouse shit? What in the name of Jesus H. Christ are you animals doing in my head?
(to JOKER)
Why is Private Pyle out of his bunk after lights out?! Why is Private Pyle holding that weapon? Why aren't you stomping Private Pyle's guts out?

JOKER
Sir, it is the private's duty to inform the Senior Drill Instructor that Private Pyle has a full magazine and has locked and loaded, sir!

HARTMAN *and* PYLE *look at each other.* PYLE *smiles from the depths of his own hell.*

HARTMAN *focuses all of his considerable powers of intimidation into his best John-Wayne-on-Suribachi voice.*

HARTMAN
Now you listen to me, Private Pyle, and you listen good. I want that weapon, and I want it now! You will place that rifle on the deck at your feet and step back away from it.

With a twisted smile on his face PYLE *points his rifle at* HARTMAN.

HARTMAN *looks suddenly calm. His eyes, his manner are those of a wanderer who has found his home.*

HARTMAN
What is your major malfunction, numbnuts?!! Didn't Mommy and Daddy show you enough attention when you were a child?!!!

BANG!

The round hits HARTMAN *in the chest.*

He falls back dead.

JOKER *and* PYLE *stand looking at the body.*

Then PYLE *looks at* JOKER *and slowly raises his rifle.*

> JOKER
> *(trembling)*
> Easy, Leonard. Go easy, man.

PYLE *breathes heavily, and keeps the rifle aimed at* JOKER.

JOKER *is scared shitless.*

PYLE *looks at* JOKER *for several seconds and slowly lowers the rifle. Then he stumbles back a few steps and sits down heavily on the toilet.*

PYLE *turns away from* JOKER *and stares into space, a strangely peaceful look transforming his face.*

He places the muzzle of the rifle in his mouth.

> JOKER
> *No!!!*

BANG!

PYLE *pulls the trigger and blows the back of his head over the white tiled wall behind him.*

SCENE FADES TO BLACK

FADE IN:

51 EXT. DA NANG STREET, VIETNAM—DAY

Motorcycles, cars, Vietnamese civilians. Swinging her hips with exaggerated sexiness, an attractive HOOKER *in a mini-skirt walks toward a café table on the pavement where* JOKER *and* RAFTERMAN *are seated.*

Music: Nancy Sinatra's "These Boots Are Made for Walking."

The girl stops at JOKER's *table.*

> HOOKER
> Hey, baby, you got girlfriend Vietnam?

> JOKER
> Not just this minute.

> HOOKER
> Well, baby, me so horny. Me so horny. Me love you long time. You party?

> JOKER
> Yeah, we might party. How much?

> HOOKER
> Fifteen dolla.

> JOKER
> Fifteen dollars for both of us?

> HOOKER
> No. Each you fifteen dolla. Me love you long time. Me so horny.

> JOKER
> Fifteen dollar too boo-coo. Five dollars each.

> HOOKER
> Me suckee-suckee. Me love you too much.

> JOKER
> Five dollars is all my mom allows me to spend.

> HOOKER
> Okay! Ten dolla each.

> JOKER
> What do we get for ten dollars?

> HOOKER
> Everything you want.

> JOKER
> Everything?

> HOOKER
> Everything.

> JOKER
> Well, old buddy, feel like spending some of your hard-earned money?

> RAFTERMAN
> Just a minute.

RAFTERMAN *raises his Nikon and starts photographing* JOKER *and the* HOOKER.

The girl strikes quick poses for the camera and coughs.

JOKER *puts his arm around her.*

> JOKER
> You know, half these gook whores are serving officers in the Viet Cong.

The girl coughs again.

> JOKER
> The other half have got T.B. Make sure you only fuck the ones that cough.

A young VIETNAMESE BOY *walks up behind* RAFTERMAN *and grabs the Nikon camera from his hands.*

The BOY *runs to an accomplice sitting on a waiting motorbike and tosses the camera to him. Then in mockery the* BOY *executes a few Bruce Lee moves before jumping on the bike and zooming off.*

JOKER *laughs.*

DISSOLVE TO:

52 EXT. U.S. MARINE BASE — DAY

*The main gates of the base. High-security fencing.
Tanks, jeeps, trucks. A military helicopter lands.*

DISSOLVE TO:

53 EXT. DA NANG BASE — DAY

*JOKER and RAFTERMAN walk down the base street
past rows of hootches and other buildings. In the
background some marines play basketball.*

> JOKER
> That little sucker really had some moves on
> him, didn't he?

> RAFTERMAN
> Yeah . . . You know what really pisses me off
> about these people?

> JOKER
> What?

> RAFTERMAN
> We're supposed to be helping them and they
> shit all over us every chance they get . . . I
> just can't feature that.

> JOKER
> Don't take it too hard, Rafterman. It's just
> business.

> RAFTERMAN
> I hate Da Nang, Joker. I want to go out into
> the field. I've been in this country almost
> three months, and all I do is take handshake
> shots at awards ceremonies.

> JOKER
> You get wasted your first day in the field and
> it'd be my fault.

> RAFTERMAN
> A high school girl could do my job. I want to
> get out into the shit. I want to get some
> trigger time.

> JOKER
> If you get killed, your mom will find me after
> I rotate back to the world and she'll beat the
> shit out of me. That's a negative, Rafterman.

54 INT. SEA-TIGER HUT — DAY

A Quonset hut. An editorial meeting of The Sea
Tiger, *the official marine newspaper, is in progress
presided over by* LIEUTENANT LOCKHART.

*JOKER, RAFTERMAN, and six other marine
correspondents are seated around a large messy
table covered with cameras, photographs,
newspapers and magazines.*

> LOCKHART
> Okay, guys, let's keep it short and sweet
> today. Anybody got anything new?

> JOKER
> There's a rumor going around that the Tet
> ceasefire is gonna be cancelled.

> LOCKHART
> Rear-echelon paranoia.

> JOKER
> A bro in Intelligence says Charlie might try to
> pull off something big during the Tet holiday.

> LOCKHART
> They say the same thing every year.

> JOKER
> There's a lot of talk about it, sir.

> LOCKHART
> I wouldn't lose any sleep over it. The Tet
> holiday's like the Fourth of July, Christmas
> and New Year all rolled into one. Every
> zipperhead in Nam, North *and* South, will be
> banging gongs, barking at the moon and
> visiting his dead relatives.

> LOCKHART
> All right . . . Ann-Margret and entourage are
> due here next week. I want someone to be
> there on the airfield and stick with her for a
> couple of days. Uh, Rafterman, you take it.

RAFTERMAN
Aye-aye, sir.

LOCKHART
Get me some good low-angle stuff. Don't make it too obvious, but I want to see fur and early morning dew.

RAFTERMAN
Yes, sir.

LOCKHART
(reading)
"Diplomats in Dungarees—Marine engineers lend a helping hand rebuilding Dong Phuc villages . . ." Chili, if we move Vietnamese, they are evacuees. If they come to us to be evacuated, they are refugees.

CHILI
I'll make a note of it, sir.

LOCKHART
(reading)
"N.V.A. Soldier Deserts After Reading Pamphlets—A young North Vietnamese Army regular, who realized his side could not win the war, deserted from his unit after reading Open Arms program pamphlets." That's good, Dave. But why say North Vietnamese Army regular? Is there an irregular? How about North Vietnamese Army soldier?

DAVE
I'll fix it up, sir.

LOCKHART
Lawrence Welk Show's gonna go out on TV in two weeks. Dave, do a hundred words on it. AFTV'll give you some background stuff.

DAVE
Yes, sir.

LOCKHART
(reading)
"Not While We're Eating—N.V.A. learn marines on a search and destroy mission don't like to be interrupted while eating chow." Search and destroy. Uh, we have a new directive from M.A.F. on this. In the future, in

place of "search and destroy," substitute the phrase "sweep and clear." Got it?

JOKER
Got it. Very catchy.

LOCKHART
And, Joker . . . where's the weenie?

JOKER
Sir?

LOCKHART
The kill, Joker. The kill. I mean, all that fire, the grunts must've hit something.

JOKER
Didn't see 'em.

LOCKHART
Joker, I've told you, we run two basic stories here. Grunts who give half their pay to buy gooks toothbrushes and deodorants—Winning of Hearts and Minds—okay? And combat action that results in a kill—Winning the War. Now you must have seen blood trails . . . drag marks?

JOKER
It was raining, sir.

LOCKHART
Well, that's why God passed the law of probability. Now rewrite it and give it a happy ending—say, uh, one kill. Make it a sapper or an officer. Which?

JOKER
Whichever you say.

LOCKHART
Grunts like reading about dead officers.

JOKER
Okay, an officer. How about a general?

A few laughs.

LOCKHART
Joker, maybe you'd like our guys to read the paper and feel bad. I mean, in case you didn't

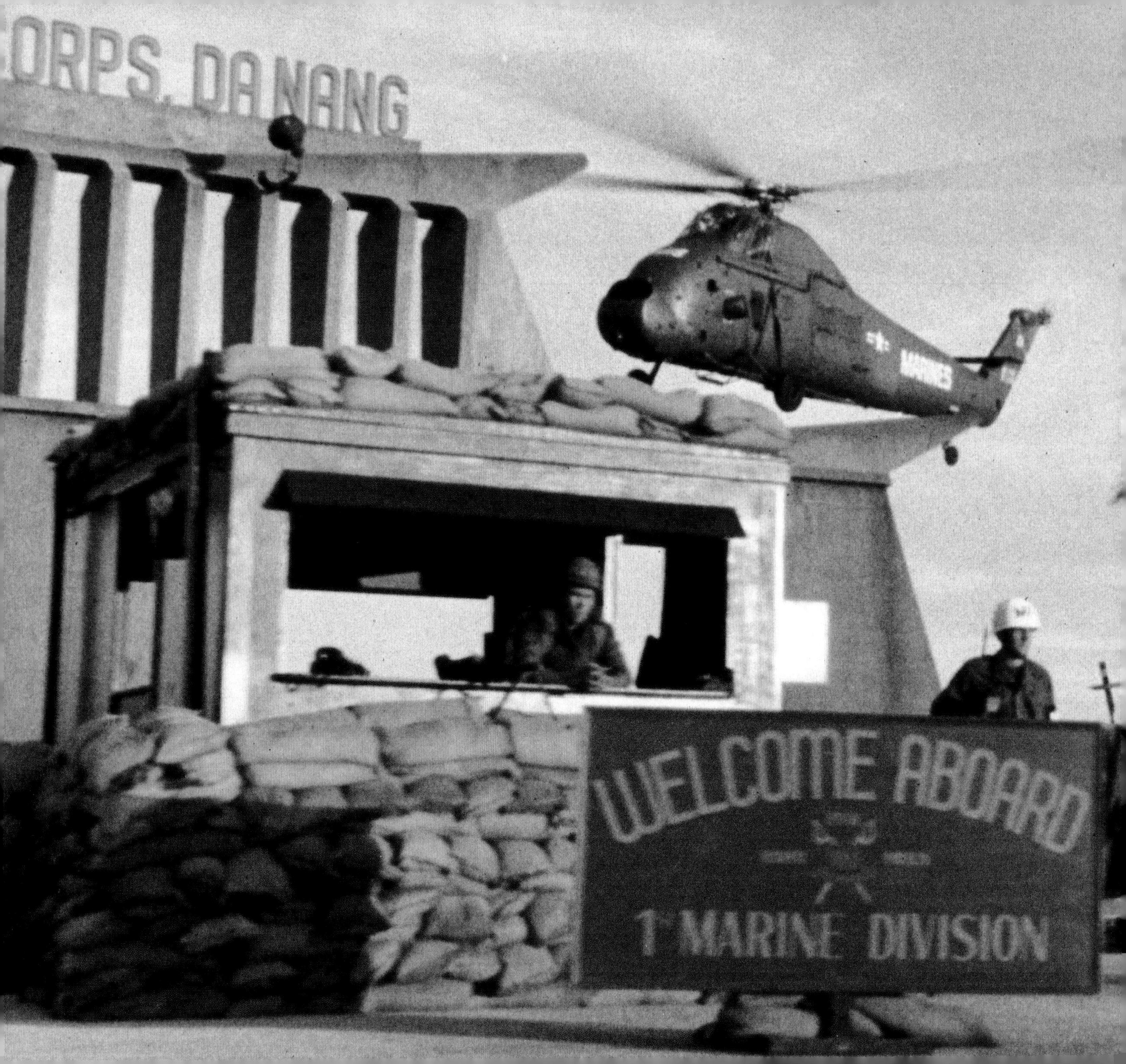
ORPS, DA NANG
MARINES
WELCOME ABOARD
1st MARINE DIVISION

know it, this is not a particularly popular war. Now, it is our job to report the news that these why-are-we-here civilian newsmen ignore.

JOKER

Sir, maybe you should go out on some ops yourself. I'm sure you could find a lot more blood trails and drag marks.

Some laughs.

LOCKHART

Joker, I've *had* my ass in the grass. Can't say I liked it much. Lots of bugs and too dangerous. As it happens, my present duties keep me where I belong. In the rear with the gear.

DISSOLVE TO:

55 EXT. DA NANG BASE—DUSK

Rows of hootches. In the distance, fireworks.

JOKER
(voiceover)

Tet. The Year of the Monkey. Vietnamese Lunar New Year's Eve. Down in Dogpatch, the gooks are shooting off fireworks to celebrate.

DISSOLVE TO:

56 INT. HOOTCH—NIGHT

JOKER, RAFTERMAN, PAYBACK *and the others are in their bunks, reading, lazing, smoking grass.* JOKER *is writing in a notebook.*

JOKER
(yawns and stretches)

I am fucking bored to death, man. I gotta get back in the shit. I ain't heard a shot fired in anger in weeks.

PAYBACK

Joker's so tough he'd eat the boogers out of a dead man's nose . . . then ask for seconds.

Some laughs.

JOKER
(John Wayne voice)

Listen up, pilgrim. A day without blood is like a day without sunshine.

PAYBACK

Shi-i—i-t! Joker thinks the bad bush is between old mama-san's legs.

Some laughs.

PAYBACK

He's never been in the shit. It's hard to talk about it, man. It's like on Hastings.

CHILI

Aw, you weren't on Operation Hastings, Payback. You weren't even in country.

PAYBACK

Eat shit and die, you fucking Spanish-American! You fucking poge! I was there, man. I was in the shit with the grunts.

JOKER
(John Wayne voice)

Don't listen to any of Payback's bullshit, Rafterman. Sometimes he thinks *he's* John Wayne.

PAYBACK

You listen to Joker, new guy. He knows *ti ti.* Very little. You know he's never been in the shit, 'cause he ain't got the stare.

RAFTERMAN

The stare?

PAYBACK

The thousand-yard stare. A marine gets it after he's been in the shit for too long. It's like . . . it's like you've really seen beyond. I got it. All field marines got it. And you'll have it too.

RAFTERMAN

I will?

STORK

Hey, Payback. How do you stop five black dudes from raping a white chick?

PAYBACK

Fuck you, Stork.

60

STORK
Throw 'em a basketball.

Laughter.

They are startled by the dull boom of mortar shells outside.

DAVE
Incoming.

PAYBACK
Oh, shit!

CHILI
They're outgoing.

DAVE
That ain't outgoing!

Some closer explosions, much louder.

CHILI
That *ain't* outgoing!

DAVE
Now what I just say?

The men grab their helmets, flak jackets and weapons and run outside.

RAFTERMAN
Joker, is this for real?

JOKER
Yes, it is, Rafterman.

57 EXT. DA NANG BASE—NIGHT

Men running everywhere. Sirens. A mortar round lands in the distance, then others nearer. Fires are breaking out.

58 INT. BUNKER—NIGHT

JOKER loads an M-60 machine gun, then hunches down watching the main gate of the perimeter.

JOKER
Hey, I hope they're just fucking with us. I ain't ready for this shit.

STORK
Amen.

The sound of a truck approaching.

The marines get set.

The truck smashes though the gates.

The marines open fire.

The truck is hit by a hail of automatic fire; it explodes and starts burning.

N.V.A. troops follow the truck through the gate.

The attackers are cut down by a withering fire from the marines.

The attack peters out.

People yell, "Cease fire."

The firing trails off.

DISSOLVE TO:

59 EXT. DA NANG BASE—DAWN

JOKER *and* RAFTERMAN *walk through the wreckage of the night's battle.*

Prisoners are led past.

LOCKHART
(voice over)
The enemy has very deceitfully taken advantage of the Tet ceasefire to launch an offensive all over the country. So far, we've had it pretty easy here. But we seem to be the exception.

60 INT. SEA-TIGER OFFICE—DAWN

Dirty and still in their combat gear, JOKER, RAFTERMAN, PAYBACK *and the other correspondents are slumped in their chairs around the table.*

LOCKHART
(walking)
Charlie has hit every major military target in Vietnam, and hit 'em hard. In Saigon, the United States Embassy has been overrun by

61

suicide squads. Khe Sahn is standing by to be overrun. We also have reports that a division of N.V.A. has occupied all of the city of Hue south of the Perfume River. In strategic terms, Charlie's cut the country in half . . . the civilian press are about to wet their pants and we've heard even Cronkite's going to say the war is now unwinnable. In other words, it's a huge shit sandwich, and we're all gonna have to take a bite.

Long, serious pause.

> JOKER
> Sir . . . does this mean that Ann-Margret's not coming?

Laughter.

> LOCKHART
> *(pissed off)*
> Joker. . . . I want you to get straight up to Phu Bai. Captain January will need all his people.

> JOKER
> Yes, sir.

> LOCKHART
> And Joker, you will take off that damn button. How's it gonna look if you get killed wearing a peace symbol?

> RAFTERMAN
> Sir? Permission to go with Joker?

> LOCKHART
> Permission granted.

> RAFTERMAN
> Thank you, sir.

> JOKER
> Sir, permission not to take Rafterman with me?

> LOCKHART
> You still here? Vanish, Joker, most ricky-tick, and take Rafterman with you. You're responsible for him.

61 EXT. HELICOPTER SHOTS—DAWN

A military helicopter flies past a huge sun.

62 INT. AERIAL HELICOPTER—DUSK

JOKER *sits looking out the door.*

RAFTERMAN *is frightened and airsick.*

The DOORGUNNER *laughs and yells as he fires his M-60 machine gun.*

We see Vietnamese below running and falling.

> DOORGUNNER
> Get some . . . get some . . . get some . . . get some . . . yeah . . . yeah . . . get some . . . get some.

After a while the DOORGUNNER *stops firing and grins at* JOKER.

> DOORGUNNER
> *(shouting to be heard)*
> Anyone who runs is a V.C. Anyone who stands still is a well-disciplined V.C.
> *(laughs)*
> You guys oughtta do a story about me sometime.

> JOKER
> Why should we do a story about you?

> DOORGUNNER
> 'Cause I'm so fucking good! That ain't no shit neither. I've done got me one hundred and fifty-seven dead gooks killed. And fifty water buffaloes, too. Them're all certified.

RAFTERMAN *gags.*

> JOKER
> Any women or children?

> DOORGUNNER
> Sometimes.

> JOKER
> How can you shoot women and children?

RAFTERMAN *gags*.

> DOORGUNNER
> Easy. You just don't lead 'em so much.
> *(laughs)*
> Ain't war hell?

DISSOLVE TO:

63 EXT. LZ HUE—DAY

The helicopter lands.

JOKER and RAFTERMAN jump out, duck down low and move away through pink smoke blown by the rotor blades.

Marines run by carrying wounded on stretchers.

> JOKER
> *(to a sergeant)*
> Top, we want to get in the shit.

> MASTER SERGEANT
> Down the road, two-five.

> JOKER
> Two-five. Outstanding! Thanks, Top.

DISSOLVE TO:

64 EXT. ROAD TO HUE—DAY

A road next to a small canal on the outskirts of Hue.

Tanks, trucks and marines are moving into the city past a column of refugees heading the other way.

JOKER and RAFTERMAN catch up to a lieutenant, salute him and walk alongside.

> JOKER
> Excuse me! Sir . . . we're looking for First Platoon, Hotel two-five. I got a bro named Cowboy there.

> TOUCHDOWN
> You people one-one?

> JOKER
> No, sir. We're reporters for *Stars and Stripes*.

> TOUCHDOWN
> *Stars and Stripes?*

> JOKER
> Yes, sir.

> TOUCHDOWN
> I'm Cowboy's platoon commander. Cowboy's just down the road in the platoon area.

> JOKER
> Oh. You mind if we tag along, sir?

> TOUCHDOWN
> No problem. Welcome aboard. By the way, my name's Schinoski. Walter J. Schinoski. My people call me Mister Touchdown. I played a little ball for Notre Dame.

> JOKER
> Notre Dame?

> TOUCHDOWN
> *(laughing)*
> Yeah.

> JOKER
> All right!

> TOUCHDOWN
> You here to make Cowboy famous?

> JOKER
> Ha! Never happen, sir.

> TOUCHDOWN
> Well, if you people came looking for a story, this is your lucky day. We got Condition Red and we're definitely expecting rain.

> JOKER
> Outstanding, sir. We taking care of business?

> TOUCHDOWN
> Well, the N.V.A. are dug in deep. Hotel Company's still working this side of the river. Street by street and house by house. Charlie's

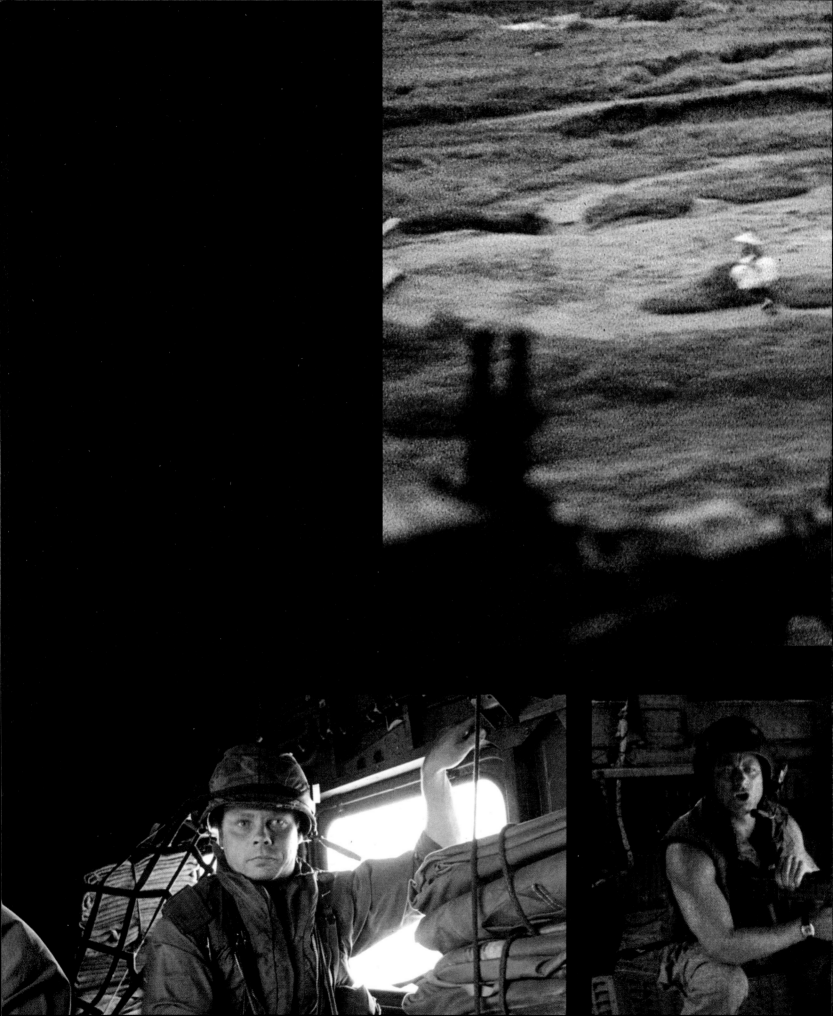

definitely got his shit together. But we're still getting some really decent kills here.

JOKER

We heard some scuttlebutt, sir, about the N.V.A. executing a lot of gook civilians.

TOUCHDOWN

That's affirmative. I saw some bodies about half a klick this side of Phu Cam Canal.

JOKER

Can you show me where, sir?

TOUCHDOWN

Here's the canal . . .

65 EXT. MASS GRAVE—DAY

JOKER *stands looking down into a large open grave at a row of white, lime-covered corpses.*

Journalists, marines and civilians are grouped around the grave.

A work detail leans on their shovels, their faces covered with bandanas against the stench.

JOKER
(voice over)
The dead have been covered with lime. The dead only know one thing. It is better to be alive.

JOKER *approaches a young lieutenant*—CLEVES.

JOKER
Excuse me. Good morning, Lieutenant.

LT. CLEVES
Good morning.

JOKER
I make it twenty. Is that the official body count, sir?

LT. CLEVES
(sharply)
What outfit are you men with?

JOKER
Sir, we're reporters from *Stars and Stripes*.

LT. CLEVES
(warms up)
Oh, I see.

JOKER
I'm Sergeant Joker and this photographer's Rafterman.

RAFTERMAN *starts shooting pictures of the lieutenant.*

LT. CLEVES
I'm Lieutenant Cleves. I'm from Hartford, Connecticut.

JOKER
Have you got a body count, sir?

LT. CLEVES
We think it's twenty.

JOKER
Do you know how it happened, sir?

LT. CLEVES
Well, it seems the N.V.A. came in with a list of gook names. Government officials, policemen, ARVN officers, schoolteachers. They went around their houses real polite and asked them to report the next day for political re-education. Everybody who turned up got shot. Some they buried alive.

A marine COLONEL *who has been watching* JOKER *turns from the group around the grave and strides up.* JOKER *snaps to attention.*

COLONEL
Marine!

LT. CLEVES
Colonel.

COLONEL
Marine, what is that button on your body armor?

JOKER
A peace symbol, sir.

COLONEL
Where'd you get it?

JOKER
I don't remember, sir.

COLONEL
What is that you've got written on your
helmet?

JOKER
"Born to Kill," sir.

COLONEL
You write "Born to Kill" on your helmet and
you wear a peace button. What's that
supposed to be, some kind of sick joke?!

JOKER
No, sir.

COLONEL
You'd better get your head and your ass wired
together, or I will take a giant shit on you!

JOKER
Yes, sir.

COLONEL
Now answer my question or you'll be standing
tall before the man.

JOKER
I think I was trying to suggest something
about the duality of man, sir.

COLONEL
The what?

JOKER
The duality of man. The Jungian thing, sir.

COLONEL
Whose side are you on, son?

JOKER
Our side, sir.

COLONEL
Don't you love your country?

JOKER
Yes, sir.

COLONEL
Then how about getting with the program?
Why don't you jump on the team and come
on in for the big win?

JOKER
Yes, sir!

COLONEL
Son, all I've ever asked of my marines is that
they obey my orders as they would the word
of God. We are here to help the Vietnamese,
because inside every gook there is an
American trying to get out. It's a hardball
world, son. We've gotta keep our heads until
this peace craze blows over.

JOKER
Aye-aye, sir.

DISSOLVE TO:

66 EXT. FIELD—DAY

JOKER *and* RAFTERMAN *walk through a field
toward a pagoda.*

67 EXT. PAGODA—DAY

*Marines are moving supplies. Some men are rest-
ing on the ground. A helicopter flies overhead.*

Music: Sam the Sham's "Wooly Bully."

JOKER
Hey, bro, we're looking for First Platoon,
Hotel two-five.

MARINE
Around the back.

JOKER *and* RAFTERMAN *walk to the back of the
building.*

JOKER
(to another marine)
First Platoon?

MARINE
Yeah, through there.

68 INT. PAGODA COURTYARD—DAY

Through a moon-door opening on to the pagoda courtyard, we see COWBOY *shaving. Other marines are sprawled around the courtyard walls.*

JOKER *walks up behind* COWBOY.

JOKER
Hey, Lone Ranger.

COWBOY
Holy shit!

JOKER
You old motherfucker.

COWBOY
It's the Joker.

JOKER
What's happenin'?

They hug each other.

COWBOY
Boy, I hoped I'd never see you again, you piece of shit!

JOKER
(laughs)
What's happening, man?

COWBOY
Oh, I'm just waiting to get back to the land of the big PX.

JOKER
Yeah? Well, why go back? Here or there, samey-same.

COWBOY
Been getting any?

JOKER
Only your sister.

COWBOY
Well, better my sister than my mom, though my mom's not bad.

COWBOY *leads* JOKER *to the center of the courtyard.*

COWBOY
This is my bro Joker from the Island. And this is . . .

JOKER
Rafterman.

COWBOY
. . . Rafterman. They're from *Stars and Stripes*. They'll make you famous.

Adlibs of "All right!"

COWBOY
We're the Lusthog Squad. We're life-takers and heartbreakers.

Adlibs.

COWBOY
We shoot 'em full of holes and fill 'em full of lead.

Adlibs of "Yeah!" etc.

A big grunt, ANIMAL MOTHER, *approaches* JOKER.

Trouble.

ANIMAL MOTHER
Are you a photographer?

JOKER
No . . . I'm a combat correspondent.

ANIMAL MOTHER
(smiles)
Oh, you seen much combat?

73

JOKER *returns the smile.*

                    JOKER
Well, I've seen a little on TV.

The other marines laugh.

                    ANIMAL MOTHER
You're a real comedian.

Some more laughs.

                    JOKER
                    (pause)
Well, they call me the Joker.

Adlibs. "Oooooooooo!" and laughter.

                    ANIMAL MOTHER
                    (moves closer)
Well, I got a joke for you. I'm gonna tear you
a new asshole.

Adlibs, laughter.

                    JOKER
                    (John Wayne voice)
Well, pilgrim ... only after you ... eat the
peanuts out of my shit!

Loud laughs and shouts.

                    ANIMAL MOTHER
                    (moves in close)
You talk the talk. Do you walk the walk?

Anticipatory adlibs of "Ooooh!" and "Whoooa!"

EIGHTBALL, *a black grunt, gets up and steps between*
JOKER *and* ANIMAL MOTHER.

                    EIGHTBALL
                    (to JOKER*)*
Now you might not believe it but under fire
Animal Mother is one of the finest human
beings in the world.

Laughter.

                    EIGHTBALL
All he needs is somebody to throw hand
grenades at him the rest of his life.

Laughter.

EIGHTBALL *leads* ANIMAL MOTHER *away.*

                    COWBOY
                    (laughing)
Come on, sit down. Come on, new guy.

EIGHTBALL *and* ANIMAL MOTHER *sit down together.*

                    ANIMAL MOTHER
Hey, jungle bunny. Thank God for the sickle
cell, huh?

                    EIGHTBALL
Yeah, mother.

CRAZY EARL *sits on the ground next to a figure
sprawled in a chair.*

                    CRAZY EARL
Hey ... photographer! You want to take a
good picture? Here, man ... take this. This
... is my bro.

CRAZY EARL *lifts the hat which has been covering
the man's face. We see he is a dead N.V.A. soldier.*

Laughter.

                    CRAZY EARL
This is his party. He's the guest of honor.
Today ... is his birthday.

Adlibs: "Happy Birthday, zipperhead!" etc.

                    CRAZY EARL
I will never forget this day. The day I came
to Hue City and fought one million N.V.A.
gooks. I love the little Commie bastards, man,
I really do. These enemy grunts are as hard
as slant-eyed drill instructors. These are
great days we're living, bros! We are jolly
green giants, walking the earth with guns.
These people we wasted here today ... are
the finest human beings we will ever know.
After we rotate back to the world, we're gonna
miss not having anyone around that's worth
shooting.

69 EXT. A FIELD, OUTSKIRTS HUE CITY—DAY

COWBOY'S *platoon, advancing towards the city in a sweep formation behind tanks.*

Cuts of the SQUAD, *nervous and alert.*

Mortar rounds explode ahead.

LIEUTENANT TOUCHDOWN *is hit and goes down.*

The platoon dives for cover.

DOC JAY *crawls to him and starts mouth-to-mouth.*

SERGEANT MURPHY *crawls up, has a look, moves to the back of the tank and picks up a field radio.*

The platoon stays flat.

> MURPHY
> Delta Six Actual, this is Murphy. Over. Delta Six Actual, this is Murphy. Over.

> DELTA SIX
> *(o.s.)*
> Delta Six.

> MURPHY
> Delta Six, we are receiving incoming fire from the ville. The Lieutenant is down. We're going to stop here and check out what's in front of us. Over.

CRAZY EARL, *keeping low, scrambles up to the* LUSTHOG SQUAD.

> CRAZY EARL
> Okay. Lusthog Squad, listen up! We're gonna move up these two roads here and check the ville. I want the third team up this road here. First and second fire team behind me up this other road, okay?

Adlibs of "Right!" and "Okay!"

> CRAZY EARL
> Let's go! Let's get it done!

Bending low, the SQUAD *moves out past the tanks, leapfrogging toward some ruined buildings a couple of hundred yards in front of them.*

HAND JOB *peers cautiously around the corner of a house and is killed instantly by a burst of automatic fire.*

ANIMAL MOTHER *opens fire with his M-60 machine gun at some windows where the shots came from.*

Everyone opens fire, blasting chunks out of the building with a zillion rounds.

T.H.E. ROCK *fires an M-79 grenade, blowing out a window.*

RAFTERMAN *photographs the action, his Nikon violently shaking.*

The fire slackens.

Then it gets quiet.

All their senses alert, everyone watches the building, listening hard.

They reload.

As CRAZY EARL *reloads he spots six V.C. dashing across the street fifty yards away. They are out of sight in a second.*

Having missed his first chance, CRAZY EARL *gets set hoping for another.*

Two more V.C. rush out into the open. He fires a long burst from his M-16 and they both go down.

CRAZY EARL *turns to the* SQUAD *with a big grin.*

Music: "Surfin' Bird" by the Trashmen. *This carries over through the next scene.*

70 EXT. LOW WALL—DAY

The platoon are hunched down behind a low wall. Tanks fire at some distant buildings. A three-man TV crew, ducking low, moves past them, filming.

> JOKER
> *(John Wayne voice)*
> Is that you, John Wayne? Is this me?

COWBOY
Hey, start the cameras. This is "Vietnam—
the Movie!"

EIGHTBALL
Yeah, Joker can be John Wayne. I'll be a
horse!

DONLON
T.H.E. Rock can be a rock!

T.H.E. ROCK
I'll be Ann-Margret!

DOC JAY
Animal Mother can be a rabid buffalo!

CRAZY EARL
I'll be General Custer!

RAFTERMAN
Well, who'll be the Indians?

ANIMAL MOTHER
Hey, we'll let the gooks play the Indians!

Laughter.

71 EXT. HUE CITY RUINS—DAY

The bodies of LIEUTENANT TOUCHDOWN *and* HAND
JOB *laid out on ground sheets. The* LUSTHOG SQUAD
*are gathered around them. The camera moves to
each man, pausing for them to speak.*

T.H.E. ROCK
You're going home now.

Camera move.

CRAZY EARL
Semper fi.

Camera move.

DONLON
We're mean marines, sir.

Camera move.

EIGHTBALL
Go easy, bros.

Camera move.

ANIMAL MOTHER
Better you than me.

RAFTERMAN
Well, at least they died for a good cause.

ANIMAL MOTHER
What cause was that?

RAFTERMAN
Freedom.

ANIMAL MOTHER
Flush out your head gear, new guy. You think
we waste gooks for freedom? This is a
slaughter. If I'm gonna get my balls blown off
for a word . . . my word is "poontang."

COWBOY
Tough break for Hand Job. He was all set to
get shipped out on a medical.

JOKER
What was the matter with him?

COWBOY
He was jerkin' off ten times a day.

EIGHTBALL
It's no shit. At least ten times a day.

COWBOY
Last week he was sent down to Da Nang to
see the Navy head shrinker, and the crazy
fucker starts jerking off in the waiting room.
Instant Section Eight. He was just waiting for
his papers to clear division.

72 EXT. HUE CITY—VARIOUS PLACES—DAY

The television crew interviews members of the
LUSTHOG SQUAD.

REPORTER
You ready?

81

CAMERAMAN
Yeah.

REPORTER
Turnover.

CAMERAMAN
Rolling.

REPORTER
Hue City interviews. Roll thirty-four.

ANIMAL MOTHER
Well . . . like, like you see, you know, it's a major city, so we have to assault with, uh . . . tanks. So, they send us in first squad . . . to make sure that there are no little Vietnamese waiting with, like, B-40 rockets that blow the tanks away. So we clear it out and we roll the tanks in and . . . basically, blow the place to hell.
(chuckles)

COWBOY
When we're in Hue . . . when we're in Hue City . . . it's like a war. You know like what I thought about a war, what I thought a war was, was supposed to be. There's the enemy, kill 'em.

RAFTERMAN
Well, I don't think there's any question about it. I mean *we're* the best. I mean all that bullshit about the Air Cav . . . When the shit really hits the fan, who do they call? They call Mother Green and her killing machine!

CRAZY EARL
Do I think America belongs in Vietnam? Um . . . I don't know. *I* belong in Vietnam. I'll tell you that.

DOC JAY
Can I quote L.B.J.?

REPORTER
Sure.

DOC JAY
(imitating L.B.J.)
"I will not send American boys eight or ten thousand miles around the world to do a job

that Asian boys oughtta be doin' for themselves."

EIGHTBALL
Personally, I think, uh . . . they don't really want to be involved in this war. I mean . . . they sort of took away *our* freedom and gave it to the, to the gookers, you know. But they don't want it. They'd rather be alive than free, I guess. Poor dumb bastards.

COWBOY
Well, the ones I'm . . . I'm fighting at are some pretty bad boys. I'm not real keen on . . . some of these fellows that are . . . supposed to be on our side. I keep meeting 'em coming the other way. Yeah.

DONLON
I mean, we're getting killed for these people and they don't even appreciate it. They think it's a big joke.

ANIMAL MOTHER
Well, if you ask me, uh, we're shooting the wrong gooks.

RAFTERMAN
Well, it depends on the situation. I mean, I'm—I'm here to take combat photos. But if the shit gets too thick, I mean, I'll go to the rifle.

ANIMAL MOTHER
What do I think about America's involvement in the war? Well, I think we should win.

COWBOY
I hate Vietnam. There's not one horse in this whole country. They don't have one horse in Vietnam. There's something basically wrong with that.
(laughs)

ANIMAL MOTHER
Well, if they'd send us more guys and maybe bomb the hell out of the North, they might, uh, they might give up.

JOKER
I wanted to see exotic Vietnam, the jewel of

Southeast Asia. I wanted to meet interesting and stimulating people of an ancient culture and . . . kill them. I wanted to be the first kid on my block to get a confirmed kill.

73 EXT. WRECKED MOVIE THEATER—DAY

The marines are seated outside the theater on rows of broken movie seats.

A motor-scooter, driven by a young ARVN *soldier with a pretty teenage Vietnamese* HOOKER *sitting behind him, and pulls up in front of the* LUSTHOG SQUAD.

The girl gets off slowly, swinging her hips as she walks.

Adlibs, hoots and hollers.

COWBOY
Ten-hut!

More hoots and hollers.

COWBOY
Good morning, little schoolgirl. I'm a little schoolboy, too.

Adlibs and laughter.

COWBOY
What you got there, chief?

The girl stands facing them, hands on hips.

ARVN PIMP
Do you want number one fuckee?

Adlibs and laughter.

COWBOY
Hey, any of you boys want number one fuckee?

Adlibs.

JOKER
Oh, I'm so horny. I can't even get a piece of hand.

DONLON
Hey! Hey! Me want suckee.

ARVN PIMP
Suckee, fuckee, smoke cigarette in the pussy, she give you everything you want. Long time.

Laughter.

COWBOY
Everything you want! All right! How much there, chief?

ARVN PIMP
Fifteen dolla each.

Adlibs: "Nooooooo!"

COWBOY
Number ten. Fifteen dolla beaucoup money.

Laughter.

COWBOY
Five dolla each.

ARVN PIMP
Come on. She love you good. Boom-boom long time. Ten dolla.

COWBOY
Five dolla.

ARVN PIMP
No. Ten dolla.

COWBOY
Be glad to trade you some ARVN rifles. Never been fired and only dropped once.

Laughter and derisive adlibs.

ARVN PIMP
(angry)
Okay, five dolla. You give me.

Adlibs.

COWBOY
Okay, okay!

86

EIGHTBALL, *a black grunt, walks up to the girl.*

> EIGHTBALL
> Let's get mounted.

> HOOKER
> *(speaks in Vietnamese)*

> ARVN PIMP
> *(argues in Vietnamese)*

> EIGHTBALL
> Something wrong there, chief?

> ARVN PIMP
> She says, uh, no boom-boom with soul
> brotha.

> EIGHTBALL
> Hey, what the mother fuck?

> ARVN PIMP
> She say soul brotha too boo-coo. Too boo-coo.

> EIGHTBALL
> Hey, what is this, man?

> COWBOY
> *(breaking up)*
> I think what he's trying to tell you is that
> you black boys pack too much meat.

Laughter.

> ARVN PIMP
> Too boo-coo. Too boo-coo.

> EIGHTBALL
> Oh, shi-i-i-t! *(laughs)* This baby-san looks
> like she could suck the chrome off a trailer
> hitch.

Laughter.

> ARVN PIMP
> She say too boo-coo. Too boo-coo.

> EIGHTBALL
> Uh, excuse me, ma'am. Now what we have
> here, little yellow sister, is a magnificent . . .
> *(takes out his dick)*

> . . . specimen of pure Alabama blacksnake.
> But it ain't too goddamn boo-coo.

The girl looks at it.

Hoots and catcalls.

> TEENAGE HOOKER
> Okay. Okay. Emjee.

More hoots.

> COWBOY
> *(mimicking Vietnamese word)*
> Okay! Okay! Emjee! Emjee!

Adlibs of "Emjee."

EIGHTBALL *starts to lead her away.*

> EIGHTBALL
> All right! This is my boogie!

> COWBOY
> Hey, we need a batting order.

ANIMAL MOTHER *grabs the girl's arm,* EIGHTBALL
holds on to the other one.

> ANIMAL MOTHER
> I'm going first.

> EIGHTBALL
> Hey, now back off, white bread. Don't get
> between a dog and his meat.

ANIMAL MOTHER *slaps* EIGHTBALL *on the wrist like
he's a naughty boy and pushes the girl into the
movie theater.*

> ANIMAL MOTHER
> *(jokingly)*
> All fucking niggers must fucking hang.

Adlibs of "Fuck you!" and laughter.

> ANIMAL MOTHER
> Hey, hey! I won't be long. I'll skip the
> foreplay.

FADE IN:

74 EXT. HUE CITY RUINS—DAY

The LUSTHOG SQUAD *on patrol moves slowly in single file, fifteen yards apart, through the ruined, smouldering city.*

> JOKER
> *(voiceover)*
> Intelligence passed the word down that during the night the N.V.A. had pulled out of our area to positions across the Perfume River. Our squad is sent on patrol to check out the report.

75 INT. BOMBED FACTORY—DAY

The patrol moves carefully through the gutted shell of a building. The clink of their gear as they walk sounds loud in the unnatural silence.

CRAZY EARL *stops to pick up a child's stuffed toy.*

BANG!

The toy triggs a booby trap, blasting CRAZY EARL *across the room.*

The SQUAD *dives for cover.*

> COWBOY
> Face outboard and take cover! Do it!

DOC JAY *scurries up to* CRAZY EARL, *who is unconscious and gives him mouth-to-mouth resuscitation.*

COWBOY *scrambles up to them. He looks at* CRAZY EARL. *Then* JOKER *runs in.*

> DOC JAY
> *(stops for a second)*
> He ain't gonna make it.

> COWBOY
> *(to himself)*
> Shit.

COWBOY *doesn't know what to do. Then he fumbles for his field radio.*

> COWBOY
> Hotel One Actual, this is Cowboy!

DOC JAY *continues the mouth-to-mouth.*

> COWBOY
> Hotel One Actual, this is Cowboy!

> MURPHY
> *(o.s.)*
> Hotel One. Over

> COWBOY
> Murph, this is Cowboy. Craze is hit. Booby trap.

> MURPHY
> *(o.s.)*
> Roger. Understand. Wait One.

COWBOY *looks around edgily.*

> MURPHY
> *(o.s.)*
> You're senior N.C.O. You take charge and continue on with the patrol. Call in at the next checkpoint. Over.

> COWBOY
> Roger. Out.

COWBOY *stares at the radio. He looks scared. He turns to* JOKER.

> COWBOY
> I'm squad leader.

JOKER *punches him reassuringly in the arm.*

> JOKER
> I'll follow you anywhere, scumbag.

DOC JAY *stops working over* CRAZY EARL *and slowly looks up.*

> DOC JAY
> He's dead.

The three men stare at the body.

76 EXT. BURNING FALLEN BUILDING—DAY

The squad moves past a burning five-storey building that has collapsed and is lying on its side.

DISSOLVE TO:

77 EXT. LOW CONCRETE WALL—DAY

EIGHTBALL, *on point, studies a map as he walks. Then he slows to a stop and signals to halt the squad.*

The squad stops and crouches down in the rubble.

EIGHTBALL *gestures for* COWBOY *to move up.*

> EIGHTBALL
> *(quietly)*
> Cowboy!

COWBOY *moves up and they kneel behind a low concrete wall.*

> COWBOY
> What's up?

> EIGHTBALL
> I think we made a mistake at the last checkpoint.

He shows COWBOY *the map.*

> EIGHTBALL
> Here . . . see what you think. I think we're here and we should be here.

COWBOY *studies the map.*

> COWBOY
> We're here?

> EIGHTBALL
> Yeah.

> COWBOY
> We should be here?

> EIGHTBALL
> Yeah . . . yeah . . . that's right.

COWBOY *is confused and scared.*

He checks his compass. Then he peers over the wall through his binoculars.

COWBOY *looks back nervously at the squad strung out behind him.*

> COWBOY
> Fuck . . . What do you think?

> EIGHTBALL
> Well, I think we should change direction.

EIGHTBALL *doesn't sound like he really knows what to do either.*

COWBOY *knows he has to make a decision.*

> COWBOY
> Okay. We'll change direction.

COWBOY *motions to the squad to come up. They rattle up and take positions behind the low wall.*

> JOKER
> What's up? ˙

> COWBOY
> Changing direction.

> JOKER
> What, are we lost?

> COWBOY
> Joker, shut the fuck up!

> COWBOY
> *(to squad)*
> Okay! Listen up! Can you hear me?

Adlibs of "Yeah!"

> COWBOY
> Okay, we're changing direction. We're heading over that way.

COWBOY *points over the wall to some ruined buildings across an open space to their left.*

90

COWBOY
Eightball's gonna go out and see if he can
find a way through.

EIGHTBALL *shrugs, apprehensively.*

COWBOY
Got it?

Adlibs of "Yeah!"

COWBOY
Eightball . . . let's dance.

EIGHTBALL *slowly gets to his knees and peers
over the wall.*

EIGHTBALL
Put a nigger behind the trigger.

78 EXT. RUINED STREET HUE—DAY

EIGHTBALL *climbs over the low wall and moves
cautiously out into the open, heading for the
damaged buildings.*

The SQUAD *covers him.*

EIGHTBALL *reaches the buildings and stops to
study the smoke-filled square.*

79 SNIPER P.O.V.—DAY

*P.O.V. from a concealed position on the second
floor of a building on the square, an AK-47 rifle is
slowly raised and aimed at* EIGHTBALL.

EIGHTBALL *turns back to wave the rest of the
squad up.*

BANG!

The SNIPER *fires.*

EIGHTBALL *is hit in the leg.*

Seen in slow motion, EIGHTBALL *twists and
crumples to the ground.*

The LUSTHOG SQUAD *fires blindly, wildly, at every
door and window in the direction of the shot.*

COWBOY
Okay, cease fire! Cease fire, goddamn it!

Some of the squad keep firing.

COWBOY
Cool it, goddamn it! Cool it! Cease fire!

Adlibs of "Cease fire!"

The firing stutters to a stop.

COWBOY
Okay, listen up! Did anybody see a sniper?
Did anybody see anything?

T.H.E. ROCK
(down the line)
Did anybody see a sniper?

DONLON
No!

DOC JAY
Nothing!

RAFTERMAN
Negative!

T.H.E. ROCK
Nothing!

Adlibs of "No!"

COWBOY
Okay, then save your ammo! Nobody fire till I
tell you!

Seen in slow motion, the SNIPER *fires again and hits*
EIGHTBALL *in the arm. He screams in pain.*

The squad opens fire at buildings facing them.

COWBOY
No, no! Cease fire! Cease fire! Animal, cease
fire!

Keeping low, DONLON *comes up and hands* COWBOY
the radio.

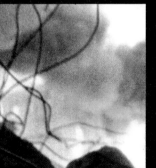

DONLON
Cowboy, it's Sergeant Murphy.

COWBOY
(into radio)
This is Cowboy. Over.

MURPHY
(o.s.)
This is Murphy. What is your present
position? Over.

COWBOY
Murph, we're receiving enemy sniper fire.
Eightball is down. Our position is about half
a klick north of checkpoint four. Believe pos-
sible strong enemy force occupying buildings
in front of us. Request immediate tank
support. Over.

MURPHY
(o.s.)
Roger. Understand. I'll see what I can do.
Over.

COWBOY
Roger. Over and out.

COWBOY
(to Donlon)
Stay close.

DONLON
Got it.

COWBOY *thinks hard for a few seconds.*

COWBOY
(to squad)
Okay, listen up! I think we're being set up
for an ambush. I think there may be strong
enemy forces in those buildings over there.
I've requested tank support. We're gonna sit
tight until it comes, but keep your eyes open.
If they decide to hit us, we'll have to pull
back fast.

The SNIPER *fires, wounding* EIGHTBALL *again, this
time in the foot. He shrieks in agony.*

Again the squad opens fire.

COWBOY
Goddamn it! Hold! Cease your fire, Mother!
Cease your fucking fire!

The firing stops.

DOC JAY
Cowboy!

COWBOY
What?

DOC JAY
We can't leave him out there!

COWBOY
We're not leaving him! We'll get him when the
tank comes up.

DOC JAY
He's hit three fucking times! He can't wait
that long!

COWBOY
I've seen this before! That sniper's just trying
to suck us in one at a time!

The SNIPER *fires and hits* EIGHTBALL *in the thigh.
His cries echo across the open space ground.*

ANIMAL MOTHER *fires madly.*

COWBOY
(shouting)
Goddamn it! No!

The squad continues firing.

COWBOY
Goddamn it, cease fire!

The firing trails off.

ANIMAL MOTHER
He's out there alone!

COWBOY
Cease fire!

The firing stops.

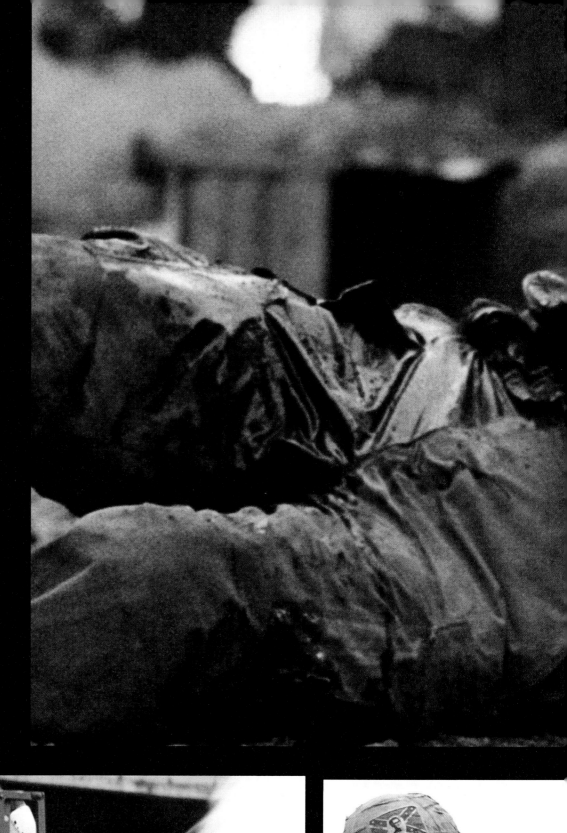

DOC JAY
Man, fuck this, fuck this shit! I'm going out to bring him in!

COWBOY
No! You stay the fuck down!

DOC JAY
Cover me!

DOC JAY *jumps over the wall and, ducking low, zigzags across the open ground.*

The squad fires to cover him.

DOC JAY *gets there safely and momentarily drops out of sight.*

COWBOY
Goddamn it! Goddamn it! Okay, cease fire! He's there!

Adlibs of "Cease fire!"

80 SNIPER P.O.V.—DAY

DOC JAY, *seen over the sights of the* SNIPER's *AK-47, drags* EIGHTBALL *toward cover.*

81 EXT. THE SQUARE—DAY

The SNIPER *fires.* DOC JAY *is hit and falls next to* EIGHTBALL.

The SQUAD *opens fire again.*

COWBOY
Hold your fire! Hold your fire!!! Cease fire! You can't see the sniper! Save the ammo! Nobody fire till I tell you! Nobody!

ANIMAL MOTHER
What the fuck do we do now, Cowboy?

COWBOY
Gimme that fucking radio.

DONLON *scuttles over with the radio.*

COWBOY
(into radio)
Murph? This is Cowboy. Over.

MURPHY
(o.s.)
This is Murphy. Over.

COWBOY
Murph, we're in some deep shit. I got two men down. What's the story on that fucking tank? Over.

MURPHY
(o.s.)
Sorry, Cowboy. No luck so far with the tank. Will advise. Over.

COWBOY
Roger. Out.
(muttering to himself)
Numbnut bastards!
(to the squad)
Okay, listen up!

T.H.E. ROCK
Listen up!

COWBOY
Can't afford to wait for the tank. I think they're gonna hit us any minute. When they do we won't have time to pull out. We gotta do it now. Let's get ready to move.

No one moves or says anything.

T.H.E. ROCK
Get ready to pull out!

ANIMAL MOTHER
Wait a minute! Hold it! Hold it! Nobody's pulling out! There's only one fucking sniper out there!

COWBOY
Back off, Mother! *I'm* calling the plays! *I* say we're pulling out!

ANIMAL MOTHER
Yeah, well, what about Doc Jay and Eightball?

100

COWBOY
I know it's a shitty thing to do, but we can't refuse to accept the situation.

ANIMAL MOTHER
Yeah, well, we're not leaving Doc Jay and Eightball out there!

COWBOY
Doc Jay and Eightball are wasted! You know that!

ANIMAL MOTHER
Bullshit! Come on, you guys! We gotta go bring 'em back! Let's go get 'em! Let's do it!

COWBOY
Stand down, Mother! That's a direct order!

ANIMAL MOTHER
Fuck you, Cowboy! Fuck all you assholes!

ANIMAL MOTHER *jumps over the wall and runs screaming and firing his M-60.*

The squad fires to cover him, blasting chunks of mortar and concrete from the buildings.

ANIMAL MOTHER
(screaming)
Fucking son-of-a-bitch! You motherfucker! Aaagh! Whooo!

ANIMAL MOTHER *reaches the buildings and drops down against a shattered wall. He calls across the open street.*

ANIMAL MOTHER
Doc! Doc! Doc! Where's the sniper?

DOC JAY *tries to speak.*

ANIMAL MOTHER
Doc, where's the sniper?

Barely able to move, DOC JAY *tries to point in the direction of the* SNIPER.

Suddenly he and EIGHTBALL *are riddled by a burst of automatic fire from the* SNIPER, *killing them instantly.*

ANIMAL MOTHER's *eyes widen in horror.*

ANIMAL MOTHER
(under his breath)
Shit!

ANIMAL MOTHER *gets to his feet and edges forward to the corner of the building.*

He carefully looks around the corner across the square at the black building, from where he thinks the shots were fired.

BANG!

A shot from the SNIPER *ricochets off the wall a few inches from his head.*

He ducks back around the corner, breathing hard.

ANIMAL MOTHER *looks around and carefully works his way to a safer spot behind another building.*

He shouts to the squad.

ANIMAL MOTHER
Hey, Cowboy!

COWBOY
Yeah!

ANIMAL MOTHER
Doc Jay and Eightball are wasted! There's only one sniper, nothing else. Move up the squad! You're clear up to here! Come on!

COWBOY *isn't sure what to do.*

COWBOY
(mutters)
Son-of-a-bitch.

The squad look to him.

He takes a couple of thoughtful breaths and decides to go.

COWBOY
Okay, listen up!

No-Doze, Stutten, Donlon, Rock—you come with me, we'll take a look! The rest of you

101

stay put and cover our ass! We may be
coming back in a big hurry!

                    JOKER
I'm going with you.

                    RAFTERMAN
I'm coming, too.

                    COWBOY
Okay.
          (To the others)
You all set?

Adlibs "Yeah!"

                    COWBOY
Let's move out!

                    T.H.E. ROCK
Let's do it!

*The five men clamber over the wall and dash
across the broken ground to the smouldering
cluster of buildings.*

When they reach ANIMAL MOTHER *he leads them
to a street off the square where they duck down
against a shattered building.*

*They catch their breath and move forward to the
next building, where they crouch down against
the wall.*

                    ANIMAL MOTHER
                    (pointing)
Cowboy . . . top of the black building,
around the corner.

COWBOY *cautiously moves to the corner of the
building and studies the strange-looking black
building which commands the square.*

*Then he ducks back around the corner, more
uncertain than ever what they should do.*

                    COWBOY
Donlon . . . give me that radio.

COWBOY *moves to* DONLON *to take the radio.*

Facing away from the black building, COWBOY *does
not notice that from the place he has moved to he
can be seen by the* SNIPER *through a jagged hole in
the building.*

83 SNIPER P.O.V. OF COWBOY

The SNIPER's *P.O.V.—* COWBOY's *upper body is just
visible through the hole in the building.*

84 EXT. SQUARE—DUSK

                    COWBOY
Murphy, this is Cowboy. Over!

A gunshot reverberates.

In slow-motion COWBOY *falls.*

                    JOKER
Cowboy!

ANIMAL MOTHER *starts firing his M-60.*

                    RAFTERMAN
                    (shouting)
Holy shit! The sniper's got a clean shot
through the hole in the wall.

*Much yelling, shouting and confusion as the men
realize where the shot came from.*

                    JOKER
                    (shouting)
Get him! Get him the fuck outta here!!

COWBOY *is carried behind the building.*

All talk at once.

                    JOKER
Easy! Easy!

                    DONLON
Get him on his back.

Adlibs.

COWBOY
(weakly)
Oh, I don't believe this shit.

Adlibs, fumbling for bandages, etc.

JOKER
Shut up! You'll be all right, Cowboy.

T.H.E. ROCK
Take it easy, Cowboy.

Four pairs of hands doing things.

COWBOY
(moaning)
Uhhh, that son-of-a-bitch!

JOKER
You're gonna be all right.

T.H.E. ROCK
You're going home, man. You're going home.

DONLON
Easy, man. Easy. Easy.

COWBOY
Ohhhh, don't shit me, Joker! Don't shit me!

JOKER
I wouldn't shit you, man. You're my favorite turd.

COWBOY *begins to lose consciousness.*

JOKER
Cowboy . . .

DONLON
Hang on, man. Hang on!

COWBOY
(coughs)
I . . . I can hack it.

T.H.E. ROCK
You can hack it.

COWBOY
I can. I—I . . .

COWBOY *spits up some blood and dies in* JOKER's *arms.*

JOKER *bends down and hugs* COWBOY.

Nobody moves.

Then, one by one, they slowly get to their feet. JOKER *is the last to get up.*

They stand looking at the body.

ANIMAL MOTHER *leaves two men to continue firing at the* SNIPER, *and he scuttles around the corner to the group around* COWBOY's *body.*

He looks at COWBOY *and then at* JOKER.

ANIMAL MOTHER
Let's go get some payback.

JOKER *looks up slowly.*

JOKER
(in cold anger)
Okay.

ANIMAL MOTHER *leads them down a narrow street.*

They stop to take cover behind a building just off the square.

They have to cross the open square, which would give the SNIPER *a clear shot at them.*

ANIMAL MOTHER
Give 'em some smoke.

He and JOKER *toss three smoke grenades into the square. They explode with a dull bang.*

They wait while the square slowly fills with smoke.

ANIMAL MOTHER *waves and they run out blindly through the thick smoke to the other side of the square.*

85 INT. BLACK BUILDING

They work their way into the shattered, burning building, past twisted steel girders and huge broken chunks of concrete.

They come to a place where they have to split up. ANIMAL MOTHER *points one way.*

> ANIMAL MOTHER
> Donlon, Rock—that way. You two with me.

DONLON *and* T.H.E. ROCK *move off as ordered.*

JOKER *and* RAFTERMAN *follow* ANIMAL MOTHER *the other way.*

They come to another place where they have to choose which way to go.

> ANIMAL MOTHER
> *(pointing)*
> Joker, in there! New Guy with me.

JOKER *cautiously enters one door.* ANIMAL MOTHER *and* RAFTERMAN *disappear through the other.*

86 INT. WRECKED AND BURNING LOBBY—DAY

JOKER *finds himself in what was the lobby of the building, a large room, which is on fire, with shattered columns, oriental arches, and windows with large decorative grillwork.*

JOKER *inches slowly into the room.*

He hears a noise, ducks behind a column and peers around it.

He sees a small, black-clad figure standing at a window—the SNIPER.

He raises his rifle, aims and squeezes the trigger.

A loud click.

In slow motion the SNIPER *turns to face* JOKER.

We see the startled face of a beautiful Vietnamese girl of about fifteen.

In slow motion JOKER *frantically works the bolt of his M-16.*

With the hard eyes of a grunt, the SNIPER *fires her AK-47 rifle.*

In slow motion JOKER *ducks behind the column, desperately trying to unjam his M-16 rifle.*

In slow motion the SNIPER *fires and runs down a few steps to get a better shot at* JOKER.

The bullets from her AK-47 tear large chunks of masonry from the column shielding him.

Suddenly the SNIPER's *body seems to explode as she is hit by a burst of automatic fire.*

RAFTERMAN *has come up and fires his M-16 into the girl's body.*

JOKER *stands trembling against the shattered column.*

RAFTERMAN *snaps another M-16 magazine into place, gestures* JOKER *to stay put, and moves forward like Supergrunt to check out the rest of the room.*

It's clear.

He moves to the window and shouts to the two men in the square.

> RAFTERMAN
> We got the sniper!

The SNIPER *lies on the floor, writhing in pain.*

JOKER *and* RAFTERMAN *cautiously approach her.*

RAFTERMAN *kicks away her AK-47.*

The two men stare at her in disbelief.

The SNIPER *is a child, no more than fifteen years old, a slender Eurasian angel with dark beautiful eyes.*

They are startled by a faint sound.

They dive for cover.

They listen.

ANIMAL MOTHER *calls from behind cover at the other end of the room.*

> ANIMAL MOTHER
> Joker?

> JOKER
> Yo.

> ANIMAL MOTHER
> What's up?

> JOKER
> We got the sniper.

RAFTERMAN *and* JOKER *circle around the* SNIPER *as* DONLON *and* T.H.E. ROCK *and* ANIMAL MOTHER *walk up.*

> RAFTERMAN
> I saved Joker's ass. I got the sniper. I fucking blew her away.

RAFTERMAN *laughs hysterically, and kisses his rifle.*

> RAFTERMAN
> Am I bad? Am I a life-taker? Am I a heart-breaker?

No one pays any attention to RAFTERMAN.

The SNIPER *gasps, whimpers.*

DONLON *stares at her.*

> DONLON
> What's she saying?

> JOKER
> *(after a pause)*
> She's praying.

> T.H.E. ROCK
> No more boom-boom for this baby-san. There's nothing we can do for her. She's dead meat.

ANIMAL MOTHER *stares down at the* SNIPER.

> ANIMAL MOTHER
> Okay. Let's get the fuck outta here.

> JOKER
> What about her?

> ANIMAL MOTHER
> Fuck her. Let her rot.

The SNIPER *prays in Vietnamese.*

> JOKER
> We can't just leave her here.

> ANIMAL MOTHER
> Hey, asshole . . . Cowboy's wasted. You're fresh out of friends. I'm running this squad now and I say we leave the gook for the mother-lovin' rats.

JOKER *stares at* ANIMAL MOTHER.

> JOKER
> I'm not trying to run this squad. I'm just saying we can't leave her like this.

ANIMAL MOTHER *looks down at the* SNIPER.

> SNIPER
> *(whimpering)*
> Sh . . . sh-shoot . . . me. Shoot . . . me.

ANIMAL MOTHER *looks at* JOKER.

> ANIMAL MOTHER
> If you want to waste her, go on, waste her.

JOKER *looks at the* SNIPER.

The four men look at JOKER.

> SNIPER
> *(gasping)*
> Shoot . . . me . . . shoot . . . me.

JOKER *slowly lifts his pistol and looks into her eyes.*

> SNIPER
> Shoot . . . me.

JOKER *jerks the trigger.*

BANG!

The four men are silent.

JOKER *stares down at the dead girl.*

> RAFTERMAN
> *(laughs)*
> Joker . . . we're gonna have to put you up for
> the Congressional Medal of . . . *Ugly!*
> *(laughs)*

JOKER *looks at* RAFTERMAN, *blankly.*

> DONLON
> Hard core, man. Fucking hard core.

87 EXT. BURNING CITY—NIGHT.

*The platoon moves through the city, silhouetted
against the raging fires. A scene in hell.*

> JOKER
> *(narration)*
> We have nailed our names in the pages of
> history enough for today. We hump down to
> the Perfume River to set in for the night.

The marines start to sing.

> MARINE PLATOON
> Who's the leader of the club that's made for
> you and me?
> M-I-C-K-E-Y M-O-U-S-E.
> Hey there. Hi there. Ho there. You're as
> welcome as can be.
> M-I-C-K-E-Y M-O-U-S-E.
> Mickey Mouse. (Mickey Mouse.)
> Mickey Mouse. (Mickey Mouse.)
> Forever let us hold our banner high.
> High. High. High.
> Come along and sing a song and join the
> jamboree.
> M-I-C-K-E-Y M-O-U-S-E.
>
> Here we go a-marching and a-shouting
> merrily.
> M-I-C-K-E-Y M-O-U-S-E.
> We play fair and we work hard and we're in
> harmony.

> M-I-C-K-E-Y M-O-U-S-E.
> Mickey Mouse. (Mickey Mouse.)
> Mickey Mouse. (Mickey Mouse.)
> Forever let us hold our banner high.
> High. High. High.
> Boys and girls from far and near you're as
> welcome as can be.
> M-I-C-K-E-Y M-O-U-S-E.
>
> Who's the leader of the club that's made for
> you and me?
> M-I-C-K-E-Y M-O-U-S-E.
> Who is marching coast to coast and far across
> the sea?
> M-I-C-K-E-Y M-O-U-S-E.
> Mickey Mouse. (Mickey Mouse.)
> Mickey Mouse. (Mickey Mouse.)
> Forever let us hold his banner high.
> High. High. High.
> Come along and sing a song and join the
> family.
> M-I-C-K-E-Y M-O-U-S-E.

> JOKER
> *(voiceover)*
> My thoughts drift back to erect nipple wet
> dreams about Mary Jane Rottencrotch and
> the Great Homecoming Fuck Fantasy. I am so
> happy that I am alive, in one piece and short.
> I'm in a world of shit . . . yes. But I am alive.
> And I am not afraid.

> MARINE PLATOON
> *(singing)*
> Come along and sing this song and join our
> family.
> M-I-C-K-E-Y- M-O-U-S-E

The marines march off into the distance.

> MARINE PLATOON
> *(singing)*
> Who's the leader of the club that's made for
> you and me?
> M-I-C-K-E-Y M-O-U-S-E
> Hey there! Hi there! Ho there!
> You're as welcome as can be.
>
> Mickey Mouse . . .

The sound fades away as the scene fades to black.

THE END

END CREDITS

Music: The Rolling Stones' "Paint It Black."

DIRECTED AND PRODUCED BY

STANLEY KUBRICK

SCREENPLAY BY

STANLEY KUBRICK

MICHAEL HERR

GUSTAV HASFORD

BASED ON THE NOVEL
The Short-Timers BY

GUSTAV HASFORD

EXECUTIVE PRODUCER

JAN HARLAN

CO-PRODUCER

PHILIP HOBBS

ASSOCIATE PRODUCER

MICHAEL HERR

ASSISTANT TO THE DIRECTOR

LEON VITALI

STARRING

PVT. JOKER	MATTHEW MODINE
ANIMAL MOTHER	ADAM BALDWIN
PVT. PYLE	VINCENT D'ONOFRIO
GNY. SGT. HARTMAN	LEE ERMEY
EIGHTBALL	DORIAN HAREWOOD
RAFTERMAN	KEVYN MAJOR HOWARD
PVT. COWBOY	ARLISS HOWARD
LT. TOUCHDOWN	ED O'ROSS
LT. LOCKHART	JOHN TERRY
CRAZY EARL	KEIRON JECCHINIS
PAYBACK	KIRK TAYLOR
DOORGUNNER	TIM COLCERI
DOC JAY	JOHN STAFFORD
POGE COLONEL	BRUCE BOA
LT. CLEVES	IAN TYLER
T.H.E. ROCK	SAL LOPEZ
DONLON	GARY LANDON MILLS
DA NANG HOOKER	PAPILLON SOO SOO
SNOWBALL	PETER EDMUND
V.C. SNIPER	NGOC LE
MOTORBIKE HOOKER	LEANNE HONG
ARVN PIMP	TAN HUNG FRANCIONE
HAND JOB	MARCUS D'AMICO
CHILI	COSTAS DINO CHIMONA
STORK	GIL KOPEL
DADDY DA	KEITH HODIAK
TV JOURNALIST	PETER MERRILL
DAYTONA DAVE	HERBERT NORVILLE
CAMERA THIEF	NGUYEN HUE PHONG
DEAD N.V.A.	DUC HU TA

LIGHTING CAMERAMAN

DOUGLAS MILSOME

PRODUCTION DESIGNER

ANTON FURST

ORIGINAL MUSIC BY

ABIGAIL MEAD

EDITOR

MARTIN HUNTER

SOUND RECORDING

EDWARD TISE

BOOM OPERATOR

MARTIN TREVIS

SOUND EDITORS

NIGEL GALT

EDWARD TISE

DUBBING MIXERS

ANDY NELSON

MIKE DOWSON

RE-RECORDING

DELTA SOUND, SHEPPERTON

SPECIAL EFFECTS SUPERVISOR

JOHN EVANS

SPECIAL EFFECTS SENIOR TECHNICIANS

PETER DAWSON

JEFF CLIFFORD

ALAN BARNARD

CASTING

LEON VITALI

ADDITIONAL CASTING

MIKE FENTON AND JANE FEINBERG C.S.

MARION DOUGHERTY

ADDITIONAL VIETNAMESE CASTING

DAN TRAN   NGUYEN THI MY CHAU

1st ASSISTANT DIRECTOR

TERRY NEEDHAM

2nd ASSISTANT DIRECTOR

CHRISTOPHER THOMSON

PRODUCTION MANAGER

PHIL KOHLER

UNIT PRODUCTION MANAGER

BILL SHEPHERD

PRODUCTION COORDINATOR

MARGARET ADAMS

COSTUME DESIGNER

KEITH DENNY

WARDROBE MASTER

JOHN BIRKENSHAW

WARDROBE ASSISTANT

HELEN GILL

CO-MAKE-UP ARTISTS

JENNIFER BOOST

CHRISTINE ALLSOP

DIALOGUE EDITOR

JOE ILLING

ASSISTANT SOUND EDITORS

PAUL CONWAY   PETER CULVERWELL

MONTAGE EDITING ENGINEER

ADAM WATKINS

VIDEO OPERATOR

MANUEL HARLAN

CAMERA TRAINEES

VAUGHAN MATTHEWS   MICHAELA MASON

EDITING TRAINEE

RONA BUCHANAN

HAIR BY

LEONARD

ART DIRECTORS

ROD STRATFORD   LES TOMKINS   KEITH PAIN

SET DRESSER

STEPHEN SIMMONDS

ASSISTANT ART DIRECTORS

NIGEL PHELPS   ANDREW ROTHSCHILD

TECHNICAL ADVISER

LEE ERMEY

ART DEPARTMENT RESEARCH

ANTHONY FREWIN

ARMOURERS

HILLS SMALL ARMS LTD

ROBERT HILLS   JOHN OXLADE

MODELLER

EDDIE BUTLER

PROP MASTER

BRIAN WELLS

CONSTRUCTION MANAGER

GEORGE CRAWFORD

ASST. CONSTRUCTION MANAGER

JOE MARTIN

PROP BUYER

JANE COOKE

COLOUR

RANK FILM LABORATORIES, DENHAM

STEADICAM OPERATORS

JOHN WARD   JEAN-MARC BRINGUIER

FOLLOW FOCUS

JONATHAN TAYLOR   MAURICE ARNOLD

JAMES AINSLIE   BRIAN ROSE

GRIP

MARK ELLIS

CAMERA ASSISTANT

JASON WRENN

CHIEF ELECTRICIAN

SEAMUS O'KANE

HELICOPTER PILOT

BOB WARREN

CONTINUITY

JULIE ROBINSON

PRODUCTION ACCOUNTANT

PAUL CADIOU

ASSISTANTS TO THE PRODUCER

EMILIO D'ALESSANDRO   ANTHONY FREWIN

PRODUCERS SECRETARY

WENDY SHORTER

PRODUCTION ASSISTANT

STEVE MILLSON

ASSISTANT ACCOUNTANT

RITA DEAN

ACCOUNTS COMPUTER OPERATOR

ALAN STEELE

PRODUCTION RUNNERS

MICHAEL SHEVLOFF   MATTHEW COLES

NURSES

LINDA GLATZEL   CARMEL FITZGERALD

SPECIAL COMPUTER EDITING PROGRAMS

JULIAN HARCOURT

UNIT DRIVERS

STEVE COULRIDGE   BILL WRIGHT

JAMES BLACK   PAUL KARAMADZA

HELICOPTER

SYKES GROUP

LABORATORY CONTACT

CHESTER EYRE

LOUMA CRANE TECHNICIAN

ADAM SAMUELSON

LOUMA CRANE AND MONTAGE VIDEO
EDITING SYSTEM

SAMUELSONS, LONDON

AERIAL PHOTOGRAPHY

KEN ARLIDGE, SAMUELSONS AUSTRALIA

OPTICAL SOUND

KAY-METROCOLOR SOUND STUDIOS

SOUND TRANSFERS

ROGER CHERRILL

TITLES

CHAPMAN BEAUVAIS

CATERING

THE LOCATION CATERERS LTD.

TRANSPORT

D&D INTERNATIONAL, DAVE CROUCHER

RON DIGWEED, CHALKY WHITE

FACILITIES

WILLIES WHEELS, RON LOWE

UNIT TRANSPORT

FOCUS CARS

ACTION VEHICLE ENGINEER

NICK JOHNS

CHARGEHAND PROP

PAUL TURNER

STANDBY PROPS

DANNY HUNTER   STEVE ALLETT

TERRY WELLS

PROPMEN

R. DAVE FAVELL CLARKE

FRANK BILLINGTON-MARKS

DRESSING PROPS

MARC DILLON   MICHAEL WHEELER

WINSTON DEPPER

SUPERVISING PAINTER

JOHN CHAPPLE

PAINTERS

LEONARD CHUBB   TOM ROBERTS

LESLIE EVANS PEARCE

RIGGERS

PETER WILKINSON   LES PHIPPS

CARPENTERS

MARK WILKINSON

A. R. CARTER   T. R. CARTER

PLASTERERS

DOMINIC FARRUGIA   MICHAEL QUINN

STAGEHANDS

DAVID GRUER   MICHAEL MARTIN

STEPHEN MARTIN   RONALD BOYD

STANDBY CONSTRUCTION

GEORGE REYNOLDS   BRIAN MORRIS

JIM COWAN   COLIN MCDONAGH

JOHN MARSELLA

PARRIS ISLAND RECRUITS AND VIETNAM PLATOON

MARTIN ADAMS	JOHN BEDDOWS	GARY CHEESEMAN	HARRY DAVIES
KEVIN ALDRIDGE	PATRICK BENN	WAYNE CLARK	JOHN DAVIS
DEL ANDERSON	STEVE BOUCHER	CHRIS CORNIBERT	KEVIN DAY
PHILIP BAILEY	ADRIAN BUSH	DANNY CORNIBERT	GORDON DUNCAN
LOUIS BARLOTTI	TONY CAREY	JOHN CURTIS	PHIL ELMER

COLIN ELVIS	ROBIN HEDGELAND	GARY MEYER	AL SIMPSON
HADRIAN FOLLETT	DUNCAN HENRY	BRETT MIDDLETON	RUSSELL SLATER
SEAN FRANK	KENNETH HEAD	DAVID MILNER	GARY SMITH
DAVID GEORGE	LIAM HOGAN	SEAN MINMAGH	ROGER SMITH
LAURIE GOMES	TREVOR HOGAN	TONY MINMAGH	TONY SMITH
BRIAN GOODWIN	LUKE HOGDAL	JOHN MORRISON	ANTHONY STYLIANO
NIGEL GOULDING	STEVE HUDSON	RUSSELL MOTT	BILL THOMPSON
TONY HAGUE	TONY HOWARD	JOHN NESS	MIKE TURYANSKY
STEVE HANDS	SEAN LAMMING	ROBERT NICHOLS	DAN WELDON
CHRIS HARRIS	DAN LANDIN	DAVID PERRY	DENNIS WELLS
BOB HART	TONY LEETE	PETER ROMMELY	MICHAEL WILLIAMS
DEREK HART	NIGEL LOUGH	PAT SANDS	JOHN WILSON
BARRY HAYES	TERRY LOWE	JIM SARUP	JOHN WONDERLING
TONY HAYES	FRANK MCCARDLE	CHRIS SCHMIDT-MAYBACH	

"Hello Vietnam"
Performed by Johnny Wright.
Courtesy of MCA Records.
Written by Tom T. Hall.
Unichappell Music Inc.
Morris Music Inc.

"The Marines Hymn"
Performed by The Goldman Band.
Courtesy of MCA Records

"These Boots Are Made for Walking"
Performed by Nancy Sinatra.
Courtesy of Boots Enterprises Inc.
Written by Lee Hazelwood,
Criterion Music Corp.

"Chapel of Love"
Performed by The Dixie Cups
by arrangement with Shelby
Singleton Enterprises
c/o Original Sound Entertainment.
Written by Jeff Barry, Ellie
Greenwich & Phil Spector.
Trio Music Co. Inc. Mother Bertha
Music Inc.

"Wooly Bully"
Performed by Sam the Sham
and the Pharaohs.
Courtesy of Polygram Special Products
a Division of Polygram Records Inc.
Written by Domingo Samudio.
Beckle Publishing Co. Inc.

"Paint It Black"
Written by Mick Jagger
and Keith Richards.
Performed by the Rolling Stones.
Produced by Andrew Loog Oldham.
Courtesy of ABKCO Music and
Records Inc.

CAMERAS BY ARRI (logo) MUNICH

fairlight®

DIGITAL AUDIO-POST MUSIC SYSTEM

Lexicon

TIME COMPRESSOR/EXPANDER

WITH GRATEFUL ACKNOWLEDGEMENT TO

DEPOT QUEENS DIVISION BASSINGBOURN

PSA BASSINGBOURN BARRACKS

BRITISH GAS PLC NORTH THAMES

THE VIETNAMESE COMMUNITY

NATIONAL TRUST NORFOLK

28633

(emblem)

MOTION PICTURE ASSOCIATION OF AMERICA

A NATANT FILM

THE END

FILMED ON LOCATION AND AT PINEWOOD STUDIOS, IVER, BUCKS

DISTRIBUTED BY WARNER BROS.

WB

A WARNER COMMUNICATIONS COMPANY

Stanley Kubrick's
FULL METAL JACKET

WARNER BROS PRESENTS STANLEY KUBRICK'S FULL METAL JACKET

STARRING
MATTHEW MODINE   ADAM BALDWIN   VINCENT D'ONOFRIO   LEE ERMEY   DORIAN HAREWOOD   ARLISS HOWARD

KEVYN MAJOR HOWARD   ED O'ROSS   SCREENPLAY BY STANLEY KUBRICK   MICHAEL HERR   GUSTAV HASFORD

BASED ON THE NOVEL THE SHORT-TIMERS BY GUSTAV HASFORD   CO PRODUCER PHILIP HOBBS   EXECUTIVE PRODUCER JAN HARLAN   PRODUCED AND DIRECTED BY STANLEY KUBRICK

A NOTE ON THE TYPE

The text of this book was set in a digitized version of Century Schoolbook, one of several variations of Century Roman. The original face was cut by Linn Boyd Benton (1844–1932) in 1895, in response to a request by Theodore Low DeVinne for an attractive, easy-to-read type face to fit the narrow columns of his *Century Magazine.*

Century Schoolbook was specifically designed for school textbooks in the primary grades, but its easy legibility quickly earned it popularity in a range of applications. Century remains the only American type face cut before 1910 that is still widely in use today.

Composition by The Sarabande Press, New York

Color separations by Colotone, North Branford, Connecticut

Printing and binding by W. A. Krueger, New Berlin and Brookfield, Wisconsin

Design and layout by Virginia Tan